Common Ground

Common Ground

A look at the beliefs Seventh-day Adventists hold in common with other evangelical Christians

Morris L. Venden

Pacific Press Publishing Association
Boise, Idaho
Montemorelos, Nuevo Leon, Mexico
Oshawa, Ontario, Canada

Printed in United States of America

Library of Congress Cataloging in Publication Data

Venden, Morris L.
Common ground.

1. Seventh-Day Adventists—Doctrines. I. Title.
BX6154.V42 1984 230'.67 84-9482
ISBN 0-8163-0564-1

84 85 86 87 88 89 • 6 5 4 3 2 1

Contents

Introduction

The purpose of this volume is to take a closer look at some of the beliefs that Seventh-day Adventists hold in common with other Bible-believing evangelical Christians. Sometimes there have been great misunderstandings among members of different faiths, and perhaps particularly so when Seventh-day Adventists have been involved. But if you check out the major beliefs and doctrines of evangelical Christians, you will discover that Seventh-day Adventists share many of the same basic beliefs.

We believe in the inspiration of the Bible. We believe that this Book is more than simply a collection of man's opinions, but that it was given by the inspiration of God through the Holy Spirit. We believe the Bible is God's Word. We believe in the Trinity—God the Father, God the Son, and God the Holy Spirit. We believe in the Bible account of creation. These beliefs which we hold in common with all evangelical Christians, we simply state here, then take for granted in the following chapters. If you have questions about these most basic truths of the Christian faith, there are books available that explain them, by C. S. Lewis, Francis Schaeffer, and others. We will begin our study in this volume by assuming at least this much of a common base in Christian belief.

A further belief that we hold in common with evangelical Christians is the conviction that mankind needs a Saviour. We believe God offers salvation to all men and that it is ours to accept. Chapter 1 begins with this truth, under the title, "The Greatest Question Ever Asked."

We believe in "A Place Called Heaven" (Chapter 2), in a life beyond this life with its sorrow and tears. We believe—with Christians of almost every denomination—that Jesus will return soon. With them, we look forward to the time "When Jesus Comes Again" (Chapter 3).

We believe in the divinity of Christ, in "Jesus, the Man Who Is God" (Chapter 4). We believe in the sinful, fallen nature of man, that we are "Sinful by Birth" (Chapter 5). We believe in the atonement of Christ, that "Christ Died for Our Sins" (Chapter 6). We believe that Jesus' sacrifice at the cross was sufficient to save anyone and that He offers this salvation freely to us, inviting us to exchange our sin for His righteousness in "The Greatest Trade Ever" (Chapter 7). Seventh-day Adventists have sometimes been charged with believing in salvation by works. Not so. We believe in salvation by faith in Jesus Christ alone.

We share the belief about "God's Enemy, the Devil" (Chapter 8) and that he walks about as a roaring lion, seeking whom he may devour. Today Christians of many faiths are coming to understand more about this spiritual warfare.

We believe in the spiritual unity and mission of the church. This subject is discussed in the final chapter, "A Lizard Can Grow a New Tail, but a Tail Can't Grow a New Lizard."

So we have a lot of *Common Ground* and invite you, whether you were born a Seventh-day Adventist or have only recently been introduced to the Adventist faith, to read these chapters and examine the truths we hold in common with evangelical Christians.

We believe in the importance of accepting God's gift of salvation

The Greatest Question Ever Asked

What is the greatest question you have ever thought of? When asked for his greatest question, Daniel Webster responded in terms of his accountability to God; but I can think of times in my life when my greatest question was merely, "Where am I going to get another dime for ice cream?"

Perhaps you have experienced this too. I remember studying to become an amateur radio operator and staying awake all night waiting for my license to come. My greatest question was, "When will my license come so I can go on the air and talk to other 'hams'?"

The greatest question of people in famine-stricken parts of the world is, "Where is the next morsel of food coming from?" Other serious questions include, "Where am I going to get a new car?" or, "How am I going to meet the next payment?" Big questions. But the *greatest* question must have something to do with our lives in terms of time and eternity.

Several years ago I attended San Francisco State College for a summer. Ninety-five percent of the students that I associated with there believed that life was here and now—and that's all. It seemed to be the sophisticated thing to believe that when we die, we're dead forever.

Frankly, I wasn't too impressed!

For a moment let's consider the question of life after death on the basis of logic and common sense. Suppose that I, as a Christian, come to you and give you a 50-50 chance that you are right, that there is nothing more than the here and now, and when you die, that's the end. You must then give me a 50-50 chance that I'm right, that heaven is a real place, and God is a real Person. In spite of the fact that I can't go into a laboratory and prove that God or heaven exists, you can't prove that they *don't* exist. So let's agree that neither of us can prove our position.

Having made this agreement, we proceed to live out our lives. When we come to the end, we discover that you were right—there is no forever. We both die, we're both buried in the same dirt. I haven't lost a thing.

But suppose that one day we look up and see in the east a small cloud. It gets bigger and bigger, and soon the whole sky is filled with heavenly beings. Christ has returned with the angels on the clouds of heaven. See Revelation 1:7. It turns out that there *is* a life beyond this life. God is real, angels are real, heaven is real. What now if you have turned it down? Why, you will have lost just about everything, for what is life here compared to eternity?

Sometimes we fail to use common sense in our perspective on life. We become so absorbed in details that we forget the total picture. We become so preoccupied with *now* that we forget about *later*.

I was invited to give the graduation address to a class of kindergarten students. It was a humongous honor. The graduates marched in, wearing homemade gowns and cardboard mortarboards with tassles hanging down, and I was supposed to try to say something! I had decided that I would have to get them involved in the address or I would never keep their attention, so I had a problem for them to solve. I said, "Let's pretend that in my left hand I have a note for one million dollars, to be paid when you are twenty-one years old. In my right hand I have a dime that you can have right now. Which would you choose?''

I could see the lollipops and ice cream bars and bubble gum going by in their minds. So I tried to appeal to them on the basis of their vast education and the fact that they were now graduates, to give careful consideration to this knotty problem. I feared what they were going to decide, so I held them off as long as possible. But when I finally asked for their answer, every one of them chose the dime! I could tell by their pleased expressions that they knew I would be impressed by their careful thinking!

Was that attitude limited to Kiddie Kampus? No, the whole world is hooked on it. We've been called the ''Now Generation.'' Until we realize a need for something beyond the here and now, we will continue to make the same type of choice as these ''graduates'' did.

It is easy to get bogged down with the narrow picture of our lives here as compared to the hereafter. Jesus told a story about a small barn and a big fool. A rich man made one mistake. He left God out of his thinking. His greatest question was, ''Where am I going to get space to store my goods?''

He concluded, ''I need to tear down my barns and build bigger ones.'' He said to his soul, ''Eat, drink, and take your ease.'' You can read the story in Luke 12. He had forgotten that God was keeping his heart beating, that God, the Author of life, was responsible for the blood flowing through his veins. He had become so self-sufficient that he believed himself responsible for keeping things going.

Do you believe that God is keeping your heart beating at this very moment? I do. No scientist in the world can produce the wonders that make up the human body. You can go to the local druggist and get all the chemicals that make up the human body. They won't cost very much. You can measure out the correct proportions, add a lot of water, and stir—and make your own human being! Right? No way!

There is not a man alive who can create a kernel of corn, let alone a human body. Oh, I've seen candy that looked like corn kernels, but you could plant them and water them until doomsday, and they'd never grow. Scientists can analyze corn and tell you exactly what ingredients are in it and in what proportions; they can even assemble these together. But they won't grow because there's still something missing—life!

Some people believe that God started life on this planet, then sort of put us on automatic pilot. But the Bible does not teach that life continues independent of God. The great God of the universe is sustaining life moment by moment. This same God invites us to consider the real issues of life.

John 3:16 tells us we have only two options. "God so loved the world that he gave his only begotten Son, that whosoever believeth in him should not perish, but have everlasting life." Just two choices—perish or live forever. Matthew 7:13, 14 describes these options as the broad way, which many choose, and the narrow way, which few find. People overlook the plan of salvation because they want to do things their own way. Salvation and eternal life have to do with a direct confrontation with the great God of the universe as revealed in Jesus Christ. The choice is made by choosing or refusing to enter into a saving relationship with Him.

In the intensive-care unit of a hospital I visited a woman who had tried to commit suicide. I was by her bed as she returned to consciousness, and I'll never forget her anger when she realized she still had to face life. She exclaimed, "I had no choice coming into this world. I ought to at least have a choice going out!"

At least she was right on the first count. None of us had a choice about coming into this world. So whose responsibility was it?

You might say, "My father and mother were responsible."

No. God is the Author of life. God! He is responsible for your being born. He is not responsible for the world of sin, but He *is* responsible for our being born here.

He is also responsible for offering us the option of a life beyond this life. God has never held us responsible for being born in a world of sin. He holds us responsible only for the choices we make concerning accepting or rejecting the plan of salvation that He has provided as His answer to the problem of sin. He is extremely patient with us as we try to understand.

The Bible states the greatest question ever asked in these words, "What shall it profit a man, if he shall gain the whole world, and lose his own soul?" Mark 8:36. I grew up seeing this text on the stage of the auditoriums where my father and uncle held evangelistic meetings. Each night, before I started making airplanes in the sawdust, I'd go through a little ritual: I'd look at those big, bold letters and follow the lines on the sign, "W-H-A-T S-H-A-L-L I-T P-R-O-F-I-T A M-A-N. . . ." The letters still burn in my vision. "What shall it profit a man, if he shall gain the whole world, and lose his own soul?"

My dad came to me once and said, "Son, I have a proposition to make you. I want to give you a million dollars."

I laughed! I knew more about my dad's bank account than to believe he could give me a thousand dollars! But he persisted. "Pretend that I'm a multimillionaire and I'm going to give you a million dollars. Are you interested?"

"Of course!"

He continued. "There are two conditions. First of all, you have to agree to spend the whole million in one year."

Well, I would have preferred to spread the fun over a longer period, but better a million for one year than no million at all.

Then he said, "The second condition is that at the end of the year, you die in the gas chamber."

I said, "I beg your pardon?"

He said, "At the end of the year, you die. There's no way out. You can't use the money to get lost on some tropical island. It is a sure thing you'll die at the end of the year. Are you still interested?"

I said, "No way!"

"Why not?"

"Because I'd be spending the whole year thinking about the gas chamber, and that would spoil all the fun."

I've tried the same proposition on many others since then, and the answer is usually the same. It is not a good deal to trade one year, even if it is a fantastic year, for a whole lifetime.

Then my father came in with the punchline, which you could expect a preacher to give his preacher's kid! My father said, "Now pretend that I am the devil and I make you a similar offer. I say, You can have 70 years to do exactly as you please. No rules, no regulations. Have fun. Live it up. But at the end of the 70 years, you will find yourself in the lake of fire with me."

Although the devil doesn't really have the 70 years to give, thousands of people have accepted his offer and think they are wise.

Most of us agree it would be foolish to settle for one year, when 70 years are available. But what about settling for 70 years when you could have eternity? It's foolish, even on the basis of logic and reason, to turn down God's offer of eternal life. Yet thousands settle for the temporary pleasures and lose eternity.

Legend has it that a scorpion wanted to cross a river. He couldn't swim, so he asked a frog to ferry him. The frog refused. "I know what you'll do," said the frog. "You'll sting me, and I'll sink to the bottom and drown."

"I wouldn't do that," insisted the scorpion. "If I did, I would drown the same as you."

The frog was finally convinced, and they started out. Sure enough, halfway across, the scorpion stung the frog. As they sank, the frog asked sadly, "Why did you do that? Now we're both going to die."

The scorpion said, "I'm sorry. I couldn't help it. It is my nature."

Because of man's nature, mankind continues to turn down eternity in favor of here and now. Even many brilliant people refuse God's offer of life and settle for life here as the total package. We are slaves to our nature, just as the scorpion was. Unless the miracle-working power of God intervenes, no amount of logic and reason can persuade us to accept God's offer.

Sometimes young people say, "What about all the fun and excitement you can enjoy if you're not tied down by a bunch of rules?"

I remember, early in my life, when a carnival came to town and everybody else was going. My brother and I thought we knew what our dad would say, but we asked him anyway.

To our surprise, he replied, "I think it's time you made your own decisions. You know how I feel about carnivals, but I'm going to leave this decision to you."

"Really? You're going to let us decide?"

"Yes."

So we went to the carnival. The first half was tremendous! Lots of fun. We spent our money like water. Tried everything. Then we began to get dizzy, sick to our stomachs. As we left, knowing that father was home praying for us, we realized that the fun was fun while it lasted, but it didn't last long.

Down with the idea that there is no fun in the
There is fun, but it doesn't last. I believe that almos

one is searching continually for things to create fun, to replace the vacuum within when the fun goes away.

The only lasting solution to our restlessness is to come to Jesus, who has said, "Come unto me, . . . and I will give you rest." Matthew 11:28.

Once in a while someone says, "I don't need God. I'm getting along fine without Him." Consider this. The question is not only, Do I need God? but also, Does God need me? Does He?

Second Corinthians 8:9 describes the sacrifice of Christ: "Ye know the grace of our Lord Jesus Christ, that, though he was rich, yet for your sakes he became poor, that ye through his poverty might be rich." If He became poor for my sake, the least I can do is to accept His riches for His sake! I don't need God? God needs me! He had enough interest to create me and to redeem me with His own life! Then shouldn't I be interested in Him for His sake?

When we see His great love for us, it becomes the most significant thing we can do to respond to that love and to offer the prayer of the psalmist: "So teach us to number our days, that we may apply our hearts unto wisdom." Psalm 90:12.

A Place Called Heaven

Would you be interested if you were given the choice to live your life over again?

Most people answer, "I sure would! I would do a lot of things differently."

No, would you like to live your life over again if you had to live it exactly as you have lived it, with all the joys, all the sorrows, everything just the same?

The more a person has seen of life, the quicker comes the reply, "No, thanks."

Most people would not be interested in living life over again in exactly the same way. Life here is usually not that inviting.

If that's true, then our greatest single reason for being here is clearly indicated by God in His Word, to accept the offer of something of better quality and greater quantity—eternal life. To accept eternal life and to help someone else accept it is our big mission here.

I am thankful that we can believe in heaven. I'm thankful that most Christian people do believe in heaven. We say so in the Lord's Prayer: "Our Father which art in heaven." We consider heaven a real place if we consider our Father real. But there are many people who do not think heaven is real. Many young people have said, "I don't care to go to heaven. There won't be anything to do there." One of them told me, "I enjoy life here, but I'm not interested in heaven whatsoever." They seemed to be sincere in that statement. But could it be that part of our problem is that we don't believe heaven is real?

A well-known actor was asked why an actor can get up and talk about something that isn't real, and people get excited about it. But a clergyman can get up and talk about something that is real, and people are completely uninterested. The reply is obvious. The actor has learned to talk about something that isn't real as though it were. And the preacher has fallen into the trap of talking about things that are real as though they are not. Which supports a premise that we learned in our speech class when we were in college, that how you say something is more important than what you say.

I wish it were possible to talk as convincingly about the things of heaven as the actor speaks about things of fiction. Only the Holy Spirit can help us with that.

Peter speaks of our hope of heaven in 1 Peter 1:3, 4: "Blessed be the God and Father of our Lord Jesus Christ, which according to his abundant mercy hath begotten us again unto a lively hope by the resurrection of Jesus Christ from the dead, to an inheritance incorruptible, and undefiled, and that fadeth not away, reserved in heaven for you."

Is the hope of heaven real to you? If Jesus is real, then heaven is real. But if Jesus is unreal to you, heaven is probably unreal as well. The London street urchin said to the skeptic, "Where Jesus is, that's heaven." Heaven was real to him.

But is Jesus real? Most people believe that He was, at least before His resurrection. Some have trouble believing that He was real flesh and bones and blood *after* the resurrection. They consider Him more of a spirit. I'd like to remind you that Jesus *was* real after the resurrection. Read Luke 24:39. The disciples thought Jesus was a ghost or spirit. Jesus asked them, "Why are ye troubled? Behold my hands and my feet, that it is I myself: handle me, and see; for a spirit hath not flesh and bones, as ye see me have."

Thomas, you remember, was a doubter. He disbelieved the testimony of the rest of the disciples, who saw Jesus. When Jesus met Thomas, He said, "Reach hither thy finger, and behold my hands; and reach hither thy hand, and thrust it into my side; and be not faithless, but believing." John 20:27.

Thomas answered, "My Lord and my God." The post-resurrected Christ was real. Flesh and bones, hands, feet, side—He was real.

Now we take that point and add to it something else, found in 1 John 3:2: "Beloved, now are we the sons of God, and it doth not yet appear what we shall be: but we know that, when he shall appear, we shall be like him; for we shall see him as he is." So we're going to be like Jesus. If Jesus is real, when we see Him face to face we will be just as real as He is. Heaven won't be a place of disembodied spirits sitting on clouds strumming invisible harps. It won't be like the man said when he saw a petrified bird sitting on a petrified tree in a petrified forest, singing a petrified song. He said, "This must be what heaven will be like."

No, according to Scripture, heaven is a real place. Here's a favorite text that is a classic, Philippians 3:20, 21: "Our conversation is in heaven; from whence also we look for the Saviour, the Lord Jesus Christ: who shall change our vile body, that it may be fashioned like unto his glorious body, according to the working whereby he is able even to subdue all things unto himself."

Most of us could stand some working over. All of us can accept the need of that tremendous change that comes at glorification, when Jesus returns. We're going to be fashioned like unto His glorious immortal body, which we have already noticed is a real, flesh-and-bones body.

So Jesus was real. When Jesus comes again we will be real. This gives us evidence that heaven is real.

When you study about the location of heaven, it is obvious that there are texts in Scripture that refer to heaven in the sky and to heaven on earth. In John 14 Jesus said, "I go to prepare a place for you. And if I go and prepare a place for you, I will come again, and receive you unto myself." Another text says we will be "caught up . . . to meet the Lord in the air." 1 Thessalonians 4:17.

We will spend a period of time at the location of heaven in the heavens. We believe that this time period is going to be 1000 years, according to Revelation 20, and that at the end of the 1000 years in heaven, the capital of the universe will be transferred to this earth. So both the statements about heaven in the heavens and heaven on earth apply.

Second Peter 3 makes it very clear that there is going to be heaven on earth, which will last for eternity. Verses 10-14: "The day of the Lord will come as a thief in the night." Notice it doesn't say that the *Lord* is going to come as a thief in the night, but that the *day* of the Lord comes as a thief in the night. Now notice the next phrase: "The heavens shall pass away with a great noise, and the elements shall melt with fervent heat, the earth also and the works that are therein shall be burned up. Seeing then that all these things shall be dissolved, what manner of persons ought ye to be in all holy conversation and godliness, looking for and hasting unto the coming of the day of God, wherein the heavens being on fire shall be dissolved, and the elements shall melt with fervent heat? Nevertheless we, according to his promise, look for new heavens and a new earth, wherein dwelleth righteousness."

This is a description of our earth being destroyed and made new again. At that time it will become the capital city of the universe—heaven on earth.

This is a very real picture. When Jesus said in John 14, "I

go to prepare a place,'' the evidence is that the place He would prepare in heaven would be real. He spoke of mansions which would fit easily in that giant city called the New Jerusalem which John saw. See Revelation 21:2.

I'd like to share with you something that came from the pen of a woman to whom Jesus was, quite obviously, a real person and heaven a real hope.

''Heaven. I am interested in that land because I have held a clear title to a piece of property there for over 65 years. I did not buy it, it was given to me without money and without price. The Donor purchased it for me at tremendous sacrifice. I am not holding it for speculation, since the title is not transferable. And it is not a vacant lot. For more than half a century the greatest Architect and Builder of the universe has been building a home for me. It will never grow old. Termites can never undermine its foundation, for it rests upon the eternal Rock. Fire cannot destroy it, floods cannot wash it away. No locks or bolts will ever be placed upon its doors, for no thieves or robbers can ever enter that place where my dwelling stands. It is complete and ready for me to enter and abide in peace eternally, without fear of being evicted.

''There may be a valley of deep shadows between the place where I live in California, and that to which I shall journey in a very short time. If I cannot reach my home in that city without passing through this valley of dark shadows, I am not afraid, because the best Friend I ever had went through the same valley a long time ago and drove away all its gloom. He has stuck by me through thick and thin since we first became acquainted 65 years ago, and I hold His promise in printed form, never to leave me nor to forsake me. He will be with me as I walk and I shall not lose my way through the valley when He is with me. My ticket to heaven has no date marked for the journey, no return coupon, and no permit for baggage.

"Just think of stepping on shore and finding it heaven, of taking hold of a hand and finding it God's hand, of breathing new air and finding it celestial air, of feeling invigorated, and discovering it immortality, of passing from storm and tempest to an unknown calm, of waking up and finding it home at last."

Let's consider the preparation made in heaven and the new earth for God's people. Jesus realizes that people are not happy unless they are active. Some of you may doubt that! When my brother and I were in collage, one day I was so tired that I said I wished I could go to bed and sleep for a week. As if to fulfill my wish, that day the pole broke on the pole-vaulting field, and I fell on my head. The doctor said, "Go to bed for a week." All I could endure was half a day!

When you go on vacation, planning to set up the cot with the mosquito netting and to sleep the whole time, by the first afternoon you're out polishing the hubcaps on your car or building a raft or damming up the creek. We used to plan to sleep till noon the first day of summer vacation, and would be up at daybreak wondering what to do. People are not happy unless they are active. Of course, we get tired when the pressure is too great. But Jesus knows that people find the greatest meaning in life when they are doing something they like to do, so He's made provision for people to be active in heaven.

Isaiah 65 describes it: "Behold, I create new heavens and a new earth: and the former shall not be remembered, nor come into mind." "I will rejoice in Jerusalem, and joy in my people: and the voice of weeping shall be no more heard in her, nor the voice of crying." "They shall build houses, and inhabit them; and they shall plant vineyards, and eat the fruit of them. They shall not build, and another inhabit; they shall not plant, and another eat: for as the days of a tree are the days of my people, and mine elect shall long enjoy the work of their hands. They shall not labour in vain, nor bring forth for trouble; for they are the seed of the blessed of the Lord, and their offspring with them."

A real place, where we build houses, plant vineyards, make gardens, heaven is for active people. God knows we need that kind of challenge. He knew it in the Garden of Eden. He placed Adam and Eve in a garden and gave them the work of caring for it.

One of the most common questions about heaven is Will we know our friends and loved ones? First Corinthians 13 says we will know each other as we are known, and we won't see through a glass darkly, but face to face. Jesus is interested in identity. One of the first things you notice when you study the city called the New Jerusalem is that on its foundations and gates are the names of people, the same names that their mothers gave them when they were born on this earth. We'll be known by our names, by our features, by the way we talk and walk.

My brother went to college two years before I did. The day I arrived, I walked down the hall in the dormitory and someone said, "Here comes a Venden."

"How did you know?"

"You walk like your brother!" We shall know, even as also we are known.

Jesus knows that people like to eat. He has made provision for eating in heaven. What are we going to eat? Well, we're going to eat fruit. Revelation 2:7: "To him that overcometh will I give to eat of the tree of life, which is in the midst of the paradise of God." How would you like to eat fruit from the tree of life? God has also made provision for us to drink. Matthew 26:24: He said to His disciples, "I will not drink henceforth of this fruit of the vine, until that day when I drink it new with you in my Father's kingdom."

Jesus has made provision for travel. Evidently a lot of traveling goes on up there. Angels are sent everywhere on missions of mercy and redemption, and God's people are going to join them in their work. Unfettered by mortality, they will wing their tireless flights to worlds afar, worlds that thrilled with sorrow at the spectacle of human woe and rang with songs of gladness at the tidings of a ransomed soul.

The angels will be quiet to let God's people tell the story straight from their own lips, of what it's like to be ransomed from a world of sin.

> Holy, holy, is what the angels sing,
> And I expect to help them make the courts of heaven
> ring;
> But when I sing redemption's story,
> They will fold their wings,
> For angels never felt the joy
> That our salvation brings.

The song writers have often talked of heaven. One of the best-known gospel songs describes it this way:

> Shall we gather at the river
> Where bright angel feet have trod;
> With its crystal tide forever
> Flowing by the throne of God?
> Yes, we'll gather at the river,
> The beautiful, the beautiful river;
> Gather with the saints at the river
> That flows by the throne of God.

There is a graphic description of the place called heaven recorded in *The Great Controversy*, page 675: "There are ever-flowing streams, clear as crystal, and beside them waving trees cast their shadows upon the paths prepared for the ransomed of the Lord. There the wide-spreading plains swell into hills of beauty, and the mountains of God rear their lofty summits. On these peaceful plains, beside those living streams, God's people, so long pilgrims and wanderers, shall find a home."

It would be selfish to want to go to heaven if the rewards of heaven were your only reason for being a Christian. But it is right to want to go to heaven. Jesus wants you there. He prayed for it in John 17:24: "Father, I will that they also, whom thou hast given me, be with me where I am." He wants each one of us to be there. And if He wants us there, that should be reason enough for us to want to be there—if we have the slightest picture of what Jesus has already done for us. Jesus has made provision for us to have happiness unsurpassed in heaven forever.

Have you ever twisted your brain out of shape trying to think of forever? I've heard it said, "I think I'd get tired of living forever." But why do we get tired here? We get tired of tears. But we've already seen in Isaiah 65 that tears are to be wiped away. We get tired of sin and its results. But Nahum 1:9 says that sin will not rise up a second time. We get tired of pain and death, but we read in Revelation 21:4 that "there shall be no more death, neither sorrow, nor crying, neither shall there be any more pain: for the former things are passed away." We get tired of sickness, but Isaiah 33:24 says, "The inhabitants shall not say, I am sick." We get tired of anxious nights, of funeral trains, of shattered hopes, of dark valleys, of loneliness, weariness, and fear, but none of these things will be there. God has provided something better. And one of the most exciting pictures of heaven is to try to understand what things aren't going to be there, which will make it so much more blessed to be there ourselves.

We live in a world where we know very little of anything that lasts. Everything we know has an end. We live in a world where people think and plan toward the day when they may be able to retire. They work hard and get the bungalow paid for, they have beautiful flowers by the front door, and curtains on the windows. And about the time their dreams are about to be fulfilled, sickness strikes. The doctor comes, hospital bills mount up, the house has to be sold to pay for the expenses. Soon all that's left is a tombstone, a monument to a broken heart.

We live in a time when the artist can become excited about painting on canvas. He paints, and as he continues his career, he learns to capture the beautiful sights around him. He can hardly pull himself away from the canvas to eat or sleep. But at the height of his career, his hand begins to shake and he has to give up.

We live in a world where the astronomer can peer into the starry heavens through ever more sensitive instruments. He studies. He spends sleepless nights looking out through the universe. And just when he is discovering the most outstanding wonders, his eye begins to grow dim and he has to sink back in discouragement.

The singer pursues her career, singing the oratorios of the masters. As she soars to the heights, the audience is spellbound. Then just when she is at her best, her voice begins to crack and she has to give up.

The businessman becomes absorbed in business. He puts all of his best energies into his growing empire. But it isn't long before he, too, finds that the golden bowl is breaking, the silver cord about to loosen, and his career ends.

People everywhere, with all of their dreams and goals and plans in this world are painfully aware that nothing lasts, nothing is forever in this life. Only in heaven will we know the meaning of eternity.

The question is, Are *you* going to be there? Oh, you may say, I'm too far from it. I'll never make it. There's not a chance in the world for me. I asked a class one time what would be the first thing they would do when they got to heaven, and one young man said, "If I got to heaven, I'd be so surprised I don't know what I'd do!"

But Ephesians 2:13 brings hope to each one of us, for it tells how we can be there: "In Christ Jesus, ye who sometime were far off are made nigh by the blood of Christ." Do you feel as if you are a long way off? Through the blood of Jesus, through His death for you, you are made near. Heaven is not something you earn, it is not something you work for. It is a gift. All you must do is receive it.

Are you saved? Can you know that you are saved now? Well, it depends on what you mean. There are three Greek words for salvation. One means, "Have I accepted the death of Jesus for all mankind?" Another, "Am I presently in a saving relationship with Jesus?" And a third, "Will I be saved some time in the future?"

Let me ask you, Have you accepted the death of Jesus for all mankind? If so, you are saved in that sense. Are you presently in a saving relationship with Jesus Christ? Are you on speaking terms with Him? Did you talk to Him today? You know the answer to that question. We don't have to worry about whether or not we will be saved at some future time. We cannot predict what we may decide in the meantime. But we can know that we are saved today, and we can continue to choose God each day. That is the big issue. Have you accepted Jesus and His blood that brings you close to heaven today? You can make that choice.

John 5:24 tells us that if we have accepted Jesus and believe in Him, we have already passed from death to life; we don't even come into judgment. First John 5:12 says, "He that hath the Son hath life; and he that hath not the Son of God hath not life." What does it mean to have the Son? Well, I say I have a wife. Why do I say I have a wife? Because I am in a meaningful relationship with her. We say, I have a wife, I have a husband, I have a friend. We mean that we have personal fellowship and communication with these people. If you have Jesus, you have accepted His salvation and are in a meaningful relationship with Him.

Jesus has provided a real place called heaven for those who will appreciate it. There are some who would be utterly miserable in heaven, and God in His great love allows them to destroy themselves. Heaven will be for those who appreciate it, because Jesus is there and they know Him and love Him. They will remember what it was like not to have heaven, and they will value their blessings in the light of what they have been through.

Someone asked a little boy to give a definition of salt. He said, "Salt is what ruins the potatoes when you don't have any."

We can take off on that and say that love is what spoils a marriage when it is missing. Smoking is what makes you healthy when you don't do it. Water is what makes you thirsty when the well goes dry. Sorrow is what makes you happy when it is no more. Tears are what bring you joy when they are wiped away. Death is what makes you glad when it is gone forever. And heaven is what makes you sad when you don't believe in Jesus.

But for those of us today who accept the promise of God's Word, we can look forward to the happiness that Jesus has provided for His people in a real place, a place called heaven.

When Jesus Comes Again

The world today is in a bad way. If I were a physician and had a patient as ill as this world is now, I would despair of being able to help him. A patient with a weak heart is not necessarily doomed to an early death. With good care and intelligent treatment, he has a good chance of living to a ripe old age. If, however, he is also afflicted with cancer and tuberculosis and perhaps pneumonia; if he should suddenly break out all over with a rash and become afflicted with typhus and typhoid, there would be little reason for hope that he would recover. And if, in addition to all this, he should have a stroke or two, it would be safe to conclude that the end was not far off.

This is the condition of the world today. Unrest is breaking out all over. Cancer is permeating the whole social fabric. Vice and dissipation are breaking down the constitution. False political and religious doctrines are poisoning the wellsprings of life. The air is contaminated with intolerance and hatred. The whole world seems on the verge of collapse. We can say that the first stroke came in the first world war; the second, and worse in the second global war. To the astonishment of many, the patient rallied, and doctors are now frantically looking for a remedy to prevent another stroke. Few people believe that civilization can survive a third. They fear it would be three times and out.

There was a time when religionists were accused of being calamity howlers and prophets of doom. Today it is the scientists and statesmen who analyze world events and predict disaster.

An American on board a ship once told a Britisher that the only solution to the world situation was empire. The Britisher was surprised and said, "I didn't know you Americans were into that. Why, if an emperor were going to solve the problems of this world, he would have to be fantastic—extremely wise and incapable of making mistakes."

The American said, "Yes, I know. And we know who He is. He's coming soon. His name is Jesus. His will be the last great global empire, and it will last forever."

Seventh-day Adventists believe in the second coming of Christ; they have taught it and preached it for a long time. It's where we got our name—Adventists. We believe it is the great hope of the world, the event toward which all civilization has marched.

Let's divide the topic this way: First of all, the fact of His coming; second, the manner of His coming; third, the purpose of His coming; and finally, the effect of His coming on different people.

One of the greatest proofs of the fact of Jesus' coming is found in Matthew 26:63, 64. Jesus was on trial before Caiaphas. False witnesses had been brought in to get him condemned to death, but Jesus held His peace. Finally the high priest, in frustration, said to Him, "I adjure thee by the living God, that thou tell us whether thou be the Christ, the Son of God." Matthew 26:63.

Jesus was under oath in this earthly tribunal. Even though He had been silent, He did not hesitate to reply now. He not only answered the high priest's question, He gave him much more. Verse 64: "Jesus saith unto him, Thou hast said." And as if that wasn't enough, He added, "Nevertheless I say unto you, Hereafter shall ye see the Son of man sitting on the right hand of power, and coming in the clouds of heaven." That could keep a high priest awake at night for many weeks. Jesus, under oath, and perhaps even for our benefit today, promised that He would come again in the clouds of heaven. How could you improve on that, to nail down the fact of His return?

Another favorite scripture that includes the good news of the second coming is Titus 2:11: "The grace of God that bringeth salvation hath appeared to all." Sometimes we Christians have gotten the idea that fulfilling the gospel commission means that the spread of the news of salvation is completely in our department. But this text says that the grace of God that bringeth salvation hath appeared *to all.* The angels of heaven, the Holy Spirit, and all the forces of the heavenly country are involved in bringing salvation to every person.

Verses 12 and 13: "Teaching us that, denying ungodliness and worldly lusts, we should live soberly, righteously, and godly, in this present world; looking for that blessed hope, and the glorious appearing of the great God and our Saviour Jesus Christ." This is just one of the many texts on the subject of Christ's second coming.

There are many texts on the subject of the first coming of Christ. The people who were wide awake and who knew their Scriptures before Jesus came the first time, were able to tell where He would be born, the circumstances of His birth, how He would be treated, that He would be sold for thirty pieces of silver—the whole thing. But there are eight times as many texts referring to the second coming of Christ as there are referring to His first coming. Jesus Himself promised to come again in John 14:1-3. He said, "I will come again."

The manner of Christ's coming is very important. The enemy of God hates the idea of Jesus' coming in power and glory, to be seen by every eye. If the devil hates anything, it is the glory that belongs to Christ. So he has projected his own manner of working onto Jesus. What is it? He's sneaky. The devil doesn't knock on the door and say, "Good morning, I am the devil." He sneaks around through the back door or through the cellar. By now he has convinced people everywhere that Jesus is going to sneak in and sneak out and that there will be many who won't even know that He has come.

To distinguish between truth and error on the manner of Jesus' coming can be very important. Here are some texts. Acts 1:11: "This same Jesus, which is taken up from you into heaven, shall so come in like manner as ye have seen him go into heaven." The disciples saw Him go—we'll see Him come. Revelation 1:7: "He cometh with clouds; and every eye shall see him," even the men who pierced Him. Matthew 24:27: "As the lightning cometh out of the east, and shineth even unto the west; so shall also the coming of the Son of man be." Matthew 25:31: He'll come with all the holy angels—and what glory that represents! Nothing is secret about Jesus' coming except the day and the hour. Read Matthew 24:36.

What does this tell us about Jesus? There's nothing secretive or sneaky about Him. When He comes, the whole world will know it. "Amid the reeling of the earth, the flash of lightning, and the roar of thunder, the voice of the Son of God calls forth the sleeping saints. He looks upon the graves of the righteous, then, raising His hands to heaven, He cries: 'Awake, awake, awake, ye that sleep in the dust, and arise!' Throughout the length and breadth of the earth the dead shall hear that voice, and they that hear shall live."—*The Great Controversy*, page 644. The living righteous are "changed, in a moment, in the twinkling of an eye" (1 Corinthians 15:52), and with the risen saints are "caught up . . . to meet the Lord in the air" (1 Thessalonians 4:17). With songs of gladness they ascend together to the city of God.

What a day! Do you believe it's coming? It is! Jesus *is* coming again. It will be the greatest event in all the history of the world, the fruition of what Jesus started long ago.

Well, what about His purpose? Why does Jesus come? This tells us something more about Jesus. He is in the habit of finishing what He's started. This is one of the things that people have been wondering about God for a long time. Scoffers have said, It's never going to happen, it's all a myth.

Several years ago my father and uncle were holding public meetings in a town. Soon after my uncle started preaching one night a man jumped up, right down near the front, turned around, and began shouting at the congregation. He said, "Don't believe what these Venden brothers are saying. They are just a couple of calamity howlers come to town to deceive you. They're talking about the end of the world, and it's never going to happen. Things continue just like they always have, and always will." He turned to my uncle and said, "You can't show me one single proof that it's going to happen!"

My uncle said, "Yes, I can! You're the most recent proof I've seen."

The man said, "What do you mean?"

My uncle began to read from 2 Peter 3:3, 4: "There shall come in the last days scoffers, walking after their own lusts, and saying, Where is the promise of his coming? for since the fathers fell asleep, all things continue as they were from the beginning of the creation."

The man slumped into his seat. Exciting things happened back there on the sawdust trail! The Lord gave the right scripture at the right time.

No, God doesn't start something and leave it undone. There's nothing more perplexing than the habit so many have of starting something and never finishing it. When Jesus begins something, He sees it through to the end. Even when He left the tomb, on the morning of the resurrection, He paused long enough to fold the grave clothes neatly. He was finished with them. He needed them no more. That tells you something about Jesus.

What is He going to finish? He will finish the great plan of redemption. He has made provision to more than make up to us for being born in this world of sin. Aren't you thankful He is able to carry His plan through to the end, to the glorious finish that is only the beginning of eternity!

Now, when we consider God's purpose for coming, we often think that His primary purpose is to save us and take us to heaven. Of course, that's part of it, and it's wonderful. Our salvation in heaven is what justification leads to. But there are larger issues than simply getting us to heaven. Can you imagine that? There are larger issues. If the only reason for me to look for Jesus to come is for me to get to heaven, if my primary reason for being a Christian is to get out of the mess I'm in, its not enough.

I read a magazine article by someone whose family had suffered a great deal after one of their members had been struck by an affliction. The author told how the family's first reaction was, "Poor us. Why did this have to happen to our family?" Then he told how their attitude gradually changed, as they tried to see something better. Phase two of the transition was, "Why did this have to happen to him?" —a concern for the one who was afflicted. Then as they continued to ponder and pray, they entered into a third stage, a concern for *all* who are afflicted in this world of trouble. So stage one was, Us. Stage two, Him. Stage three, Everyone.

The writer said that when they got to the third step, their troubles were over. Anyone who stays in the first stage, simply concerned for himself, finds that his problems go on forever.

We can see a similar progression in our relationship to

this world of sin. The first reaction of the one who comes to realize that he lives in a world gone wrong may be, "Why did this have to happen to me? Why did I have to be born here?" But God will help that poor sinner realize a concern for others. His misery will change to compassion as he looks out on a world of trouble and tragedy.

But there's a bigger issue yet. Why God? Why the broken heart of Jesus? Pondering that question, we can experience a concern for Them up there. The plan of salvation, the gospel and restoration include all of this.

Maturity in the Christian life creates complete selflessness. No more is there rivalry and jealousy. No more anxiety about one's personal salvation. No more fearfulness about getting to heaven, or not getting there. Heaven is within, where Christ now dwells, and the rewards are in the spirit and companionship of Jesus even now. The second advent is desired, not for selfish personal benefit, but as a remedy for the woes of the world.

The complete Christian is willing, as was his Master, to give up his eternal life for the salvation of others. Eternal life? Yes. Oh, you say, Who could qualify for that? Moses did. You remember Moses. When two million mob-frenzied people wanted to crush him, he was concerned for them. But he was also concerned for God—for God's name, God's image, God's reputation.

Moses said, "Lord, save these people. And if you can't, then please blot my name out of Your book of life." He was willing to give up his eternal life. That's mature Christianity. He was far more concerned for God and for others than for his own skin, even his own eternity.

We can be thankful that God will bring an end to the whole story of sin for our sake, yes; and for the sake of the millions of others who suffer in this world of sin, yes—and also for the sake of truth and the reputation of God throughout the universe. Those who, in spite of heartache and pain and tears still love and trust God, play a significant part in vindicating God before the universe.

Well, what about the effect of Christ's second coming? How is it going to affect you and me? Let me remind you that when Jesus was here the first time, He went into the temple one day and cleansed it. The panic-stricken thieves and cheats threw their money to the winds and ran. But another group stayed behind, the little children and the aged, the helpless and the needy.

Just as there was a difference in reaction in the days when Jesus first came, so there will be a difference when He comes again. Some who have never prayed to God will pray to nature, pray to the rocks and mountains, saying, "Fall on us and hide us." See Revelation 6:14-17. But others will look up and say, "This is God. We knew He was coming, and we've been looking for Him." See Isaiah 25:9.

When Jesus was here, those who were sick and afflicted, who realized their need of His grace, were healed when He came to them.

One sat alone beside the highway begging,
His eyes were blind, the light he could not see;
He clutched his rags and shivered in the shadows,
Then Jesus came and bade his darkness flee.

Unclean! Unclean! the leper cried in torment,
The deaf, the dumb, in helplessness stood near;
The fever raged, disease had gripped its victim,
Then Jesus came and cast out every fear.

So men today have found the Saviour able,
They could not conquer passion, lust, and sin;
Their broken hearts had left them sad and lonely,
Then Jesus came and dwelt Himself within.

When Jesus comes the tempter's power is broken;
When Jesus comes the tears are wiped away.
He takes the gloom and fills the life with glory,
For all is changed when Jesus comes to stay.

Yes, when Jesus comes it will be different. We'll throw away our glasses, our canes and crutches, our hearing aids and all the things that have dragged us down. We'll be made new. As one evangelist said it, When Jesus comes we will have perfect minds in perfect bodies and live in a perfect world, and when we've lived a million years, we'll just have gotten started.

Jesus is coming again to receive us unto Himself. On that day there will be two parties. Some, after the door is shut, will want to go in. They will say, "Lord, open unto us. We want to come in."

The response will be heard, "What have you done that you should go in? What right have you to enter?"

"Oh," they will reply, "we are acquainted with You. We have eaten and drunk in Your presence, and You have taught in our streets. Besides that, we have prophesied in Your name. We have cast out devils, and we have done many wonderful works. Lord, is that not evidence enough? Open the door."

What is the answer? "Depart from me, ye that work iniquity." You can read it in Matthew 7:21-23. What did they say? WE have done many wonderful works. WE are all right. WE have a right to be there. But what WE have done won't count for much on that day.

There will be another company that day, a great multitude that no one can number, from all nations and kindreds and tongues and people. They will come to the gate of the city to enter in.

The question will be heard, "What have you done that you should enter here? What claim do you have?"

And they will answer, "Oh, we have done nothing at all to deserve it. We are sinners, dependent only on the grace of the Lord. We were so wretched and completely captive and in such bondage that no one could deliver us but the Lord Himself. We were so blind that no one but the Lord could cause us to see, so naked that no one could clothe us but Jesus. All the claim we have is what Jesus has done in our behalf. When in our wretchedness we called on Him, He delivered. When in our misery we wept, He comforted us. When in our poverty we begged, He made us rich. When in our blindness we asked Him to show the way, He led us. When we were so naked that no one could clothe us, He gave us these garments we have on.

"So all we have to present, any claim that would allow us to enter is only what He has done. If this is not enough, we are left out, and that will be just. If we are left out, we have no complaint to make. But oh, will this not entitle us to enter and possess the inheritance?"

The Heavenly Witness will answer, "Why, yes. We are perfectly satisfied with you. The deliverance you obtained from your wretchedness is that which our Lord wrought. The garments you have on the Lord gave you. The Lord wove them, and they are all divine. They are Christ's. Why, yes, you can certainly come in."

Then over the gates will come a voice of sweetest music, full of the gentleness and compassion of our Saviour. "Come, ye blessed of the Lord, why standest thou without?" The gate will swing wide open, and we shall have an abundant entrance into the everlasting kingdom of our Lord and Saviour, Jesus Christ.

Jesus, the Man Who Is God

A teenage girl said to me, "I kind of like Jesus, but I don't like God." Have you ever felt as she did? Have you ever seen Jesus as kind, friendly, and approachable, but God as harsh and judgmental? Have you ever looked at some of the Old Testament stories and wondered at the apparent difference between the God they describe and the "gentle Jesus, meek and mild" of the New Testament?

Let me remind you—Jesus *was* God. Jesus *is* God. John 1 says that He was with God from the beginning, and He was God. As such, He possessed the power of God within Him, including the power to lay down His life and take it again. See John 10:17, 18. The devil knew Jesus had the power of God within Him and even tried to persuade Him to turn stones into bread. See Matthew 4:3.

Jesus came to reveal His Father. John 14 relates how Jesus sat with His disciples in the upper room the night before His crucifixion. Philip asked Him to show them the Father. Jesus replied, "Have I been so long time with you, and yet hast thou not known me, Philip?" The Father and I are the same. "He that hath seen me hath seen the Father." Verse 9. He continued in verse 10: "Believest thou not that I am in the Father, and the Father in me? the words that I speak unto you I speak not of myself: but the Father that dwelleth in me, he doeth the works."

So who did the works in Jesus' life, according to His own statement in John 14:10? Sure, it was Jesus' hands, feet, eyes, and mouth, but somehow it was His Father doing all of it through Him, in Him. Not even His words were His own. See John 12:49.

Therefore, when we examine the life of Jesus and see His kindness and love and concern for all mankind, we are simply seeing, in clearer focus, a picture of what God the Father has always been like and always will be like.

Let's go back for a moment to an Old Testament text (Isaiah 9:6) that is obviously speaking of someone special for which no human being could ever really qualify. "Unto us a child is born, unto us a son is given: and the government shall be upon his shoulder: and his name shall be called Wonderful, Counsellor, The mighty God, The everlasting Father, The Prince of Peace." That description was certainly fulfilled in the person of Jesus Christ, wasn't it?

In the New Testament, Colossians 2:9 says of Christ, "In him dwelleth all the fulness of the Godhead bodily." So you have the Old Testament prediction that One would be born who would be the mighty God, and you have the New Testament statement that in Christ dwelled all the fullness of the Godhead bodily—two short excerpts showing us that Jesus was God.

Let's take a closer look at John 1, probably one of the best-known passages on the divinity of Christ. Here the apostle John refers to Jesus as "the Word." Begin with verse 1: "In the beginning was the Word, and the Word was with God, and the Word was God. The same was in the beginning with God. All things were made by him; and without him was not any thing made that was made." Have you ever thought about the fact that Jesus was the Creator? The One we call Jesus was the Creator of this world in the beginning. Read verse 10: "He was in the world, and the world was made by him, and the world knew him not. He came unto his own, and his own received him not. But as many as received him, to them gave he power to become the sons of God, even to them that believe on his name." Verse 14: "The Word was made flesh, and dwelt among us, (and we beheld his glory, the glory as of the only begotten of the Father,) full of grace and truth."

We are reminded here that Jesus was God, He was the Creator who made all of us, and yet He became flesh and dwelt among us. So even though Jesus was God, He was also man. In fact, He became a man forever. See Daniel 7:13; Revelation 1:13; Revelation 14:14. He is the Son of God; He is also the Son of man. As you study the book of Revelation, you discover that Jesus went back to heaven as the Son of man and is referred to as the Son of man after He had ascended to heaven.

The Bible says that God is a Spirit (John 4:24) and that the angels are spirits (Hebrews 1:14). But the Bible says that Jesus, in His resurrected form, had flesh and bones. He said, "A spirit hath not flesh and bones, as ye see me have." Luke 24:39.

Perhaps you have seen or heard of the film about the antkeeper. The basic premise of the film, appealing to boys and girls, is this: Imagine yourself looking down into a hill of ants. You like ants, and as you study their anthill, you discover that a terrible disease has broken out among them. It's going to destroy them all. The only way they can be saved is for you to become an ant yourself and effect their salvation.

The question is asked, Would you be willing to do that? The boys and girls usually say, "Yes, of course. Then when we are finished being an ant, we could go back to what we were before."

But no, they are told, "If you become an ant, you would have to stay an ant forever. Are you willing?" The children are not so quick to answer this time.

It is a great mystery just how much of an eternal sacrifice Jesus made when He came to earth and became one of us, but the Bible makes it very clear that He is still a human being in heaven. Yet He was always God, the mighty God, the Wonderful One, the mighty Counselor, the man who is God—and He always will be!

How can this be explained? How can a person be God and man at the same time? Is He half God and half man? No, the only way you could say it would be to say that He is *all* God and *all* man. It's hard to understand. But one of the most fascinating things about Jesus' life is the realization that even though Jesus was God, and even though when He became man He was *still* God, He did not live as God. It's a point worth dwelling on.

Jesus' life is the greatest example of total, absolute surrender, of submission by His own choice. His divinity remained quiet throughout His life on earth, and He submitted to His Father's control. His Father spoke the words and did the works in and through Him. Jesus did not rely upon, nor did He use, the divine part of His nature to live His perfect life. Remember He said, "I can of mine own self do nothing." See John 5:19, 30. If He had been talking about potential, it would not have been an accurate statement. As God, He could have done plenty—things that you or I could never conceive of doing. He could have done them on His own, apart from dependence upon His Father. Jesus *could* have used His inherent power, but He came to earth to show us how to live through dependence upon a higher power.

Let's take a little longer look at the temptation of Jesus as recorded in Luke 4. Jesus had been in the wilderness alone, fasting for almost six weeks. Satan appeared to tempt Him to turn stones into bread. He knew that Jesus had been born with the kind of power by which He could have done it, even without depending upon His Father.

What was the issue of the temptation? We often say appetite, but that wasn't the primary issue. It's not wrong to be hungry for bread after having fasted for six weeks. The issue was not to do something wrong. No, the devil wanted Jesus to do something right, but by using His inherent divinity instead of relying upon His Father. Satan tempted Him to prove His own divinity, to work on His own, independent of His Father. Jesus refused, saying in effect, "I am here to demonstrate to man how to live through complete dependence upon a higher power. My Father has not seen fit to supply Me with bread yet, and if it is His will that I starve to death, that's all right with Me. In the meantime, until He sends Me bread, I'll go hungry. I will not rely on My own power."

It was natural for Jesus to do good, outwardly and inwardly. He had no propensities to evil. Evil was repulsive to Him. Jesus loved righteousness and hated iniquity. See Hebrews 1:9. Therefore, the "bad" that Satan tempted Him to do was to utilize His own powers to do something good. But the fantastic truth is that He did not rely upon Himself; therefore, all of His works came from His Father.

Since Jesus hated iniquity, Satan wouldn't have gotten very far trying to tempt Him to commit sins—how could you be tempted to commit sins if you hated them? But Jesus was tempted to *sin,* on what the real issue in sin is, to go independent of God, to depend on Himself, and to do what He did in His own strength. That's the real issue in sin.

That's what happened in heaven when Lucifer fell. He decided that he didn't need to depend upon God, that he was big enough to go on his own. It's what happened in the Garden of Eden. Eve fell for Satan's temptation to become as a god and depend on herself. See Genesis 3:5. The issue in what we might call sin, singular—the basic issue in all transgression—is separation from God, going independent of God. The results of that are all the sin*s*, plural, or wrong actions and transgressions and sinful deeds that follow.

But in Jesus' life, from the cradle to the grave, even though He was constantly tempted to live on the basis of the power that was within Him, Jesus continued to depend upon His Father.

Even in His death on the cross, Jesus would not save Himself. What would have happened if we had been in His place, at His trial, when they spat and slapped and jeered and thrust the thorns deeper into His brow? How easy it would have been to say, "It's about time these people found out who it is they are pushing around!" But Jesus had not come to save Himself, so neither in Gethsemane nor during His trial nor at Calvary nor at any other time did He ever tap His divine power to save Himself or to relieve His suffering and anguish.

When the priests at the foot of the cross wagged their heads at Him and said, "He saved others, himself he cannot save," it was the truth. It was the gospel in one sentence.

If you study everything usually considered a demonstration of Christ's divinity, you will discover that His followers did the same things—opening the eyes of the blind, casting out devils, healing the sick, walking on water, reading people's minds. The greatest proof of His inherent divinity was not what He did; it's what He said, and what His Father said about Him. Jesus *spoke* as God on occasion (see John 4:26), and His Father testified to His Sonship (see Matthew 3:17; John 12:28). But He *lived* as a man. Christ in His life on earth lived in submission to God's control. He lived and worked and overcame sin and the devil in human nature, relying upon God for power.

We must never define sin and temptation primarily in terms of behavior. The issue is not of doing right and not doing wrong—but of *relationship*. Christ's temptations were not like ours in the sense that He found sinning desirable (as we often do), but most profoundly like ours in a much more basic sense: The devil constantly tempted Him to break the relationship of dependence and submission to His Father and to "go it alone" on His own strength. Indeed, this was a more severe temptation for Him than for us, since He actually *had* the greater power to do so.

The remarkable thing about Jesus' life was what He *didn't* do but which He had the power to accomplish. It was a difficult task for Him to continue to live in moment-by-moment dependence upon His Father, yet that's what He did, leaving us an example of how we may live in dependence upon His strength instead of upon our own.

How did Jesus maintain His life of submission to His Father's control? In the hours of solitary prayer and communion with His Father He received wisdom and power. How often we see Him going aside from the crowds that thronged Him day by day, to seek time alone with His Father. Mark 1:35 is one example. His disciples observed His habit of communion with His Father and thus learned where His strength lay. It was from these hours spent with God that Christ came forth to work for the salvation of mankind.

Jesus was divine, and He was human. He took upon Himself the weakness of our human nature, even though His *spiritual* nature was sinless, as Adam's had been before the fall. He lived His life in the same way in which we are to live, thus leaving us an example of dependence and trust in a power higher than ourselves.

As we think of Him who was born in a stable and died on a cross, and who is still today speaking peace to troubled hearts, may we not exclaim,

All hail the power of Jesus' name!
Let angels prostrate fall;
Bring forth the royal diadem,
And crown Him Lord of all!

Sinful by Birth

You don't have to "sin" to be sinful. All you have to do to be sinful is to be born! Jesus told Nicodemus, as recorded in John 3, that unless he was born again, he couldn't even see the kingdom of heaven. Obviously there was something wrong with his first birth.

Romans 5:12 and 19 remind us that "as by one man sin entered into the world, and death by sin, so death passed upon all men, for that all have sinned. For as by one man's disobedience, many were made sinners, so by the obedience of one shall many be made righteous." Now I like the last part of that verse! I don't like the first part, but it is still a Bible truth.

Whether we ever sin or not is beside the point. We *are* sinful. Our hearts are evil and we cannot change them. That's the condition of everyone who is born in this world.

We could go through a long list of texts to prove this point. For example, Romans 3:10: "There is none righteous, no, not one." 1 John 5:17: "All unrighteousness is sin." 1 John 1:8: "If we say we have no sin, we deceive ourselves." Ephesians 2:3: "We are by nature the children of wrath." Romans 7:18: "I know that in my flesh dwelleth no good thing." These texts are not talking about people after the age of 6 or 12 or 18. We are all sinners. We are born sinful.

This leads to a problem for some, because they say, "Do you mean that sin is in the genes and chromosomes?" No, I don't think we have evidence enough to prove that point, although some people want to. The Augsburg Confession was not too far off. I'd like to take at least a *similar* position, if you don't identify it as the *same*. It is this, basically, and I'm paraphrasing—that we are born separated from God. Being born separated from God is the basic issue in being born sinful. We would remain separated from God, without any hope, if it hadn't been for the cross. But because of the cross, we do not have to remain separated from God. God gives every one of us the option to be born again.

The first symptom of being born separated from God is that we are born self-centered. That's our problem. We're all self-centered. From this self-centeredness all that we call "sins" spring. All of our wrong deeds and actions spring from self-centeredness.

Now something else. This self-centeredness, apart from God, will continue and does continue. There is no such thing as self-centeredness being taken away apart from Jesus. As we grow older, we sometimes learn to mask our self-centeredness, but it is always there. Perhaps it would be well to remind ourselves that none, even of the apostles and prophets, ever claimed to be without sin. Men who have lived the nearest to God, men who would sacrifice life itself rather than knowingly commit a wrong act have confessed the sinfulness of their nature. We cannot say that we are sinless.

So we are sinners by birth, and we continue that way, whether we're sinning or not. We sin because we are sinful. We are not sinful because we sin—*we sin because we are sinful*.

One of the proofs that we are all sinners is that we all die. You can't argue with that, can you? I mentioned that once at a university, and one of the professors spoke up from the back, "Birds die. Cats and dogs die too. Are they sinners?"

Yes! I heard a couple of sinners fighting in the woods just the other night. They had four legs and fur. What was their problem? They were self-centered. You watch animals. They're self-centered. The problem of sin has permeated all creation. It's survival of the fittest—it's just that simple.

Birds die. Cats die. Dogs die. We had a dog once that I think was a Christian! He was the most selfless dog I have ever seen. For a long time after he died our children would go to his grave and weep. But we realize that we live in a world that has been heavily tainted by the problem of sin. Sin permeates all of creation.

What is our reason for dwelling on this point? Just this: If our hearts are evil, self-centered, and we cannot change them, and if they will continue to be so apart from Christ, then how could we ever obey God's requirements? It's a good question, isn't it? If in our flesh dwells no good thing, how can we obey?

Some people think it's impossible for us to obey. They point to our sinful natures and say that the best we can hope for is that Jesus' merits will be put to our account in heaven, and thus we will have hope of life eternal while we continue to fall and fail and sin until Jesus comes again. But is that what the Bible teaches?

In Matthew 7:16, 17 Jesus asks a very practical question: "Do men gather grapes of thorns, or figs of thistles? Even so every good tree bringeth forth good fruit; but a corrupt tree bringeth forth"—what kind of fruit?—"evil fruit." Some people say, If an evil tree cannot bring forth good fruit, how can we ever hope to obey? It's a worthwhile question.

Another way to ask the question is this: Can people who are sinful by nature ever bring forth good fruit? The answer is beautifully stated in Isaiah 61:3. I like it—see if you don't like it too. "To appoint unto them that mourn in Zion, to give unto them beauty for ashes, the oil of joy for mourning, the garment of praise for the spirit of heaviness; that they might be called trees of righteousness, the planting of the Lord, that he might be glorified."

So the Bible speaks of trees of righteousness that the Lord Himself plants for His own glory. This gives us a glimpse of hope. There is a possibility for bad trees to bring forth good fruit, if the miracle of what Jesus is suggesting here in these words of Scripture is a reality.

Let's follow that a little more closely. We have already noticed the fact that we are born sinful and must be born again to see the kingdom of God. That's an even more mighty evidence than the fact that we all die. If no one can see the kingdom of God unless he is born again, there was something wrong with his first birth.

This leads us to the question, What is new about the new birth? I would like to give you a composite definition of the new birth that tells us what's new about it. The new birth is a supernatural work of the Holy Spirit (see John 3:5), and this supernatural work of the Holy Spirit produces a change of attitude toward God (Ezekiel 36:26: "A new heart . . . will I give you"). Before the new birth a person is not interested in the things of God; he is actually against God. Romans 8:7: "The carnal mind is enmity against God: for it is not subject to the law of God, neither indeed can be." There's no joy in communion with God before the new birth. If you find a person who doesn't like to read the Bible, doesn't want to pray, doesn't want to go to religious meetings, wouldn't be caught dead in church, the problem could be that he's never been born again and has never even received the capacity for understanding and appreciating the love of God.

After sin entered, mankind could no longer find joy in holiness and tried to hide from the presence of God. Such is still the condition of the unrenewed heart. It is not in harmony with God and finds no joy in communion with Him. The sinner would not be happy in God's presence. He would shrink from the companionship of holy beings. Were he permitted to enter heaven, it would have no joy for him. It would be a place of torture.

Have you ever considered it an evidence of the love of God that He allows sinners to be destroyed? It ends their misery. He doesn't force them to go to a place that would be only torture to them.

So before the new birth, we're not interested in God, and it is only through the supernatural work of the Holy Spirit that we have a change of attitude toward Him.

The third thing the new birth does is create a new capacity for knowing and loving God that we didn't have before. First Corinthians 2:13, 14 says that spiritual things are spiritually discerned.

It is with a sense of relief that a pastor is able to talk about his children when they have grownup and left home, because when they are still around, he can always expect to get all kinds of objections from them at home after he mentions them in a sermon! My boy was in high school. He hadn't surrendered his life to Christ yet. I was worried about him. I tried to talk to him about it but didn't feel I was getting anywhere.

The one day some of the kids at school said to him, "Why don't you come with us on Wednesday night? We're going to have a Bible discussion." Well, he liked these kids, so he said, "OK, I'll go." But he said to himself, "I'll go and ask a bunch of hard questions." He enjoyed asking hard questions.

He went to the meeting, and the discussion began. For the first half he asked his hard questions. When the meeting was about halfway through, something seemed to say to him, "Venden, why don't you shut up? You might learn something." He was the only one playing his game.

He found out later that some of these kids were praying for him. I like that!

He began to listen. Before the evening was over, he heard something that he had never heard before. Oh yes, he had been told it many times! But he had never heard it with his mind. He heard that we never change our lives in order to come to Christ. We come to Him just as we are, and He's the One who changes our lives.

The miracle happened. He came home, and he could hardly stand still. He said, "Dad! Listen! I learned something tonight. We never change our lives in order to come to Christ. We come just as we are—and He loves to have us come just as we are—"

I didn't want to ruin it for him, so I said, *"Really?"*

I don't know how much he slept that night, but the next day he was reading his Bible—his Bible that we'd given him that had gathered dust. Now it was open and he was reading it. He couldn't put it down. I walked by the door and said to myself, "Praise the Lord! It has happened! It's the miracle of the new birth." He had a new capacity for knowing and loving God that wasn't even there before.

My first impression was to be insulted because I wasn't the one— But that's cheap. I was glad there was someone!

This new capacity for knowing and loving God *leads to* a willing obedience to all of His requirements and commands. And please put emphasis on the words *leads to*. In spite of the hazards carried with that emphasis, we have to underscore it because there have been too many people, including young people, who have had the idea that if you're really converted you will have a complete change of life overnight, and if you have any failures or mistakes or fallings again then you must not be converted. Please—conversion is the beginning. It isn't the end—it's the beginning.

This new heart *leads to* a new life. Mark 4:28: "First the blade, then the ear, after that the full corn in the ear." Jesus

Himself gives opportunity for growth. Let's never forget it. The prodigal son who turned his face toward his father's house had a long way to go to get to his father's house, but he was headed in the right direction.

He had a change of attitude toward his father when in the pigpen he turned toward his father's house, instead of running away. I believe he was converted there, for after that he saw something good about his father instead of all bad.

So the four-part definition of conversion is this: (1) A supernatural work of the Holy Spirit (2) produces a change of attitude toward God and (3) creates a new capacity for knowing God that we didn't have before, and (4) this *leads to* obedience. John 14:15: "If ye love me, keep my commandments."

This new life is preserved only by continual connection with Christ. I'd like to remind you that there is no such thing as righteousness apart from Jesus. Whether it's imputed or imparted is beside the point. We don't have to get into that issue at all, because there's no such thing as righteousness apart from Jesus.

Some of us preachers have been struggling to find the best way to express this concept. It isn't that humans *have* a sinful nature—it is that we *are* sinful by nature. To say that we have a sinful nature suggests that there is some sort of entity in us that we must get rid of, like perhaps a tumor that a surgeon could remove, and then we'd be all right. But it isn't that way. We are sinful by nature. WE must be changed. Do you follow?

Therefore, when we say we become partakers of the divine nature, perhaps we ought to take a second look at this old idea that has floated around for a long time, that there is an entity called a divine nature that is put in us. Perhaps you have heard this idea, that we have these two natures inside us, one fighting the other. No, we are sinful by nature, and when we are born again we are given the opportunity of becoming partakers of the divine nature. It isn't a nature that's put in us, inherently, but rather we become partakers of Christ's nature.

So you have a single, whole person, not someone who has a compartment for this and a compartment for that. He is a whole person who is either living by the nature that he was born with or living by partaking of the divine nature through connection with Christ.

Since there is no such thing as righteousness apart from Jesus, then the only way we can be trees of righteousness, planted by the Lord and nourished by the Lord, is to have begun that relationship with Him and to continue that relationship with Him. Sinful man can find hope and righteousness only in God, and no human being is righteous any longer than he has faith in God and maintains a vital connection with Him.

That's why we are invited to abide in Christ, and that's why the real issue in sin is living a life apart from Christ.

Let's try to put this together in some sort of conclusion. If we are sinners by nature, we are never going to be able to produce any obedience. And if we are the ones who are doing the living in the Christian life, we can produce only thorns and thistles. If *we* are the ones working the works, what we produce will always be imperfect.

This brings us to a crucial point—a big divide between two schools of thought that are becoming more pronounced. In the Christian life, do *we* do the living, or does Christ do the living in us? What do we mean by that? Just this much for now: When Paul said, "I am crucified with Christ; nevertheless I live; yet not I, but Christ liveth in me" (Galatians 2:20), was he saying something that is worth our attention and thought? He said, "The life which I now live in the flesh I live by the faith of the Son of God, who loved me, and gave himself for me." It is possible for Christ to dwell in our hearts by faith. See Ephesians 3. That God and Christ live in us through the power of the Holy Spirit is good Bible teaching.

Some of us went through a careful study of the gospels recently to find out what Jesus said on the subject. We found again and again this concept of the indwelling Christ, Christ living His life in us.

Which leads us to this question: If Christ was living His life in Paul, was Christ living an imperfect life? Is what the Holy Spirit does in a person going to be imperfect?

Paul says that the just shall live by faith. See Galatians 3:11. If those who have been justified through the righteousness of Christ are taking to their hearts the Scripture, "Unto us [are given] exceeding great and precious promises; that by these ye might be partakers of the divine nature, having escaped the corruption that is in the world" (2 Peter 1:4), is that imperfect? Is Christ's indwelling and living His life in us imperfect, or can it be genuine obedience?

Then do we obey? Well, in a sense, no. Christ obeys in us and through us. That's His purpose. But do you see the great divide? If a person says that we are put right with God only by our faith in what Jesus has done on the cross, but we *live* the Christian life by doing the works of righteousness, to some degree, ourselves, then it's true that there is only one thing we can produce—imperfect obedience, which is disobedience.

But if a person says we are put right with God only by what Jesus did at the cross, and we live the daily Christian life through Jesus, and Jesus only, and with Him dwelling in us, then we can have obedience that is real and genuine.

In spite of our weakness, in spite of our misunderstanding, and in spite of the fact that we are sinful by nature, Jesus has promised, "Him that cometh to me I will in no wise cast out." John 6:37. It *is* still true that Jesus loves to have us come to Him, just as we are, and that He does not require us to change our lives before we come. He wants us to come to Him so that *He* can change our lives. He will make us what He wants us to be.

When we come to Him and accept His invitation to allow Him to live His life in us, we become partakers of His divine nature, and through His power we are changed into His likeness, into His image.

thought. Apparently, the soldiers placed a person against the cross sideways, so that his feet were side by side against the cross, and then they drove a huge spike through both heels, just in front of the Achilles tendon. The soldiers drove this spike with such force that archaeologists found in one coffin a body that, when jerked off the cross after death, brought a huge chunk of wood with it. The wood and the spike and the heels were all together in the coffin.

After the soldiers had secured the body tightly to the cross sideways at the feet, they swung the shoulders around, stretched the arms out tight, and nailed them to the cross through the wrists. I tried standing in that position after I heard about it, and it wasn't long before my muscles began to jerk. When you put all this together and realize that it was God's Son who became subject to such a death, it will move your heart. It certainly moved mine.

People have sometimes reacted against the blood and gore of the cross, insisting that we should spend our time on the deeper issues involved. But we need to face the fact that there was blood and there was pain.

If anyone reacts against the emotionalism often used in altar calls, with the soft lights and music, you are not alone in that reaction. But it would be tragic to forget the reality of the cross and the fact that Jesus, with His divine/human nature, suffered every pain and insult in as much greater degree as His nature is greater than ours.

In spite of all the abuse, when Jesus was nailed to the cross, He prayed, "Father, forgive them; for they know not what they do." Luke 23:34.

Do I love Him today for what He did for me? After I try to visualize His sufferings, I am deeply moved. Yet we must not forget that in spite of all the physical pain and torture, so great was His agony of soul that the physical pain was hardly felt. He suffered untold anguish bearing the weight of our sin. Let's try to understand more of the deeper issues involved at the cross, that broke His heart and caused Him to die.

Isaiah 53, beginning with verse 4: "He [Jesus] endured the suffering that should have been ours, the pain that we should have borne. All the while we thought that his suffering was punishment sent by God. But because of our sins he was wounded, beaten because of the evil we did. We are healed by the punishment he suffered, made whole by the blows he received." Verses 4, 5, TEV.

The concept that Christ died for our sins can be found throughout Scripture. In spite of the fact that some voices today want to minimize that necessity, Christ died for our sins. He was wounded for our transgressions; and as a substitute and surety for sinful man, Christ suffered under divine justice. It was because He was our substitute and surety and bore the weight of our sin, that His physical pain was hardly felt.

But the term "divine justice" has led some people to a problem. They ask, "Do you mean that God is out looking for blood, needing to be appeased? Was Jesus trying to calm God down because He was angry?"

As it is worded in Isaiah 53, "All the while we thought that his suffering was punishment sent by God." Did God look down into a world of sin and say, "I want a pound of flesh; I want to see a sacrifice"? Is that the way God is?

In reaction against this heathen concept, some have wanted to do away with the idea of an atonement and a sacrifice completely. They look at the cross and say, "Couldn't God have forgiven us without all that?" In the attempt to present a loving God in place of an angry God who needs to be appeased, some have leaned toward the "moral influence" theory, which says the cross is not necessary for our salvation, that Jesus' death was incidental, more of a martyrdom than anything else. They say that Jesus came solely for the purpose of showing us how much God loves us and that the idea of a divine justice that must be met is mistaken. So the dialog goes on.

In order to try to solve this problem, I'd like to suggest two important factors. One, God is a God of justice, and since Jesus was God, Jesus was also a God of justice. Second, we need to understand why justice is necessary.

Anyone who has studied government knows that a government stands only so long as the government has laws. No law is any stronger than the penalty for breaking it, and no penalty is effective unless it is applied.

This is true whether you're talking about the government of the universe, the government of the United States of America, the government of a school or institution, or the government of your own home. The parent who stands at the bottom of the stairs and shouts, "This is the last time I'm going to say 'this is the last time' " has already lost the battle. His rules are obviously worth nothing, for they are not being enforced and no penalties are being applied. Without government and law and penalty you have anarchy.

God is the originator of justice. It is His very name and character. So it is because the law could not be set aside, because God's character could not be changed, because the penalty could not be ignored, that justice had to be met. But often when we think of cold justice we forget about mercy, and that is the other side of God's character that we must not neglect.

While I was a pastor in Oregon I was delayed at an appointment, which made me late to a funeral service. I was driving on a back road, spraying gravel and dust everywhere desperately trying to reach the funeral in time. Behind me rose a second cloud of dust from which emerged a law enforcement officer.

When he stopped me, he was angry. He said, "Who are you anyway? I thought I had a stolen car here."

I explained who I was and where I was going, and then he

became confused. He said, "I don't know what to do with you. If I give you a citation, it'll show up in the newspaper tomorrow and your parishioners will all know about it. And I don't think a citation is the answer anyway."

I said, "No, I don't either!"

Finally he decided to let me go and said, "Go ahead. You're on your own." As I started down the road, I thought, "This is the greatest motivation I've ever had for wanting to obey the law." There had been other times when I had not been treated mercifully. I knew what justice meant, so mercy was worth something to me.

This is a feeble illustration, and if we were going to make it more like the atonement, we'd need to have the officer do more than simply let me go, because God does more than that. God has never been able just to forgive sin. He forgives sinners, but He has never forgiven sin. We know this is true because Jesus had to die. So if my illustration were to fit, the officer on the dusty road would have gone to court for me and paid my fine from his own wallet.

So we are faced with this question of justice. God has never gone flabby when it comes to justice. Aren't you thankful for that? The entire universe can be thankful for it! How terrible it would be to live in a universe where there was no justice. Anarchy would reign everywhere! But because God is a God of love, He is also a God of justice as well as a God of mercy.

Satan didn't understand that. When he found himself outside the gates of heaven, he was Exhibit A of the fact that God is a God of justice. He came up with a clever plan that went like this: Since God is a God of justice, I must get man to sin. If mankind sins, it will prove my point that God's law is impossible to obey. I will gain control of mankind and set up my own kingdom. Then if there is some loophole and mankind is forgiven, God will have to let me back into His kingdom as well.

The devil did not know that a plan of redemption had been devised before the foundation of the world. When the emergency arose, Jesus, who was God and is God, came to this earth and by His life and death proved that God's justice does not destroy His mercy, nor does mercy destroy justice. Sinners could be forgiven and the law remain righteous.

I'd like to list briefly several things that Christ accomplished by His death on the cross.

1. He proved that God's love for man is infinite.
2. He paid the penalty for sin.
3. He proved that the law could not be changed or set aside.
4. He proved that the penalty for sin was fair and just.
5. He proved the awfulness of sin.
6. He purchased the right to forgive the sinner and still be just.
7. He made grace available to all who believe and trust in Him.
8. He redeemed us from the curse of the law.
9. He obtained the keys to the grave, the right to raise the dead.
10. He proved the wages of sin are death.
11. He made the Sabbath a memorial of creation *and* redemption.
12. He vindicated the character of God before the universe.
13. He proved that God's government will stand forever.
14. He brought back the lost dominion.

All of this and more was accomplished by Jesus' death upon the cross.

In conclusion, I'd like to invite you to consider the sacrifice of Jesus once again as written by my son Lee when he was a college freshman.

"Do you know what it's like to be lonely? So alone that

none but your own thoughts are ever your companions? Do you know what it's like to be a child and want to play with other children but meet only ridicule? Do you know what it's like to wish for a retreat in the quiet of your own home, but even there to find laughter and sarcasm?

"Do you know what it's like to spend hours, days, and nights in the lonely refuge of mountain or desert? Do you know what it's like to sit high on a lonely hill, overlooking a city, wishing you could be someone's friend? Do you know how it feels to sleep on rough ground without a blanket, night after night?

"Have you ever walked through a crowd, attended a dinner party, or passed through a marketplace teeming with people, and yet somehow still felt alone? Have you ever watched from the shadows while friends laughed and talked? Have you ever stood on the sidelines while others enjoyed an activity or game? Have you ever been invited by someone to get acquainted, and then been told to come after dark so no one would see you together? Have you ever been turned away, no matter what town you went to, or who you asked for lodging? Have you ever returned to your hometown acquaintances, seeking to give friendship, and had rocks thrown at you? Do you know how it hurts to have no one to talk to, no one to share with, no one who will even listen?

"Have you ever cried so hard that your eyes ached, and trying to talk you could only moan between sobs? Have you ever spent entire nights in tears that no one will ever know about except you? Have you ever thought you had found a few who accepted you as their friend, and then watched as they left or ignored you so as not to be embarrassed by you? Have you ever felt the pain of rejection or the bitter disappointment of broken trust? Have you ever given of yourself until there was nothing left to give, and then heard mocking laughter because you were so vulnerable?

"Have you ever struggled against giving up the effort to give yourself, struggled until you actually sweat blood? Have you ever spent entire nights worrying and praying for a troubled friend? Have you gone to that same friend for comfort and understanding yourself and heard him say, 'I'm too tired to talk to you.'

"Have you ever been rudely jostled by calloused men? Have you ever had someone spit on your bruised and bleeding face? Have you ever felt blood trickle down your back from your own torn flesh? Have you ever felt the sharp pain of thorns forcefully pressed deep into your scalp and temples by rough men? Do you know how it feels to struggle through your own blood drops while dragging heavy timbers? Do you think you could stagger on, willingly, dying for those who hate, despise and reject you?

"Could you bear screaming insults, laughter, and mocking as you collapsed beneath your instrument of death? Would you struggle desperately to rise and continue toward your place of execution? Have you ever felt the grinding, tearing crunch of nails being pounded through your hands and feet? Have you ever felt with every nerve of your body the jolt and thud of a cross dropping into its deep, ugly hole?

"Have you ever hung from wounds gaping ever wider while crowds taunted you and threw rocks at your bruised and lacerated body? Have you ever gasped hoarsely for breath, aware that you were dying? Have you ever felt that even your own father had forsaken you? Do you know how it feels to have vision grow dim as your eyes glaze? Have you ever exhaled your last breath, knowing that it is finished?

"Have you ever hurt? Have you ever ached? Have you ever suffered? Have you ever died, alone, for those who refused to let you be their friend?

"While on earth, Jesus did. And all the time, He longed for companionship and communication. He still does.

"Won't you be His friend?"

We believe in justification by faith in Christ alone

The Greatest Trade Ever

I would like to make you an offer. I have a ballpoint pen that I would like to trade for a Cadillac Seville. If any of you has that sort of car and is willing to trade with me for my ballpoint pen—which is a perfectly good ballpoint pen!—either you are stupid or you really love me a lot! One of the two.

Have you ever done any "horse-trading"? Did you ever do any trading when you were a child—things like marbles or bubble-gum cards? I used to trade when I was in the back alleys of New York City, in Brooklyn. We would trade bubble-gum cards with the other kids. We used to trade three little marbles for one big one. For many of us, this sort of thing continues throughout life. We had a necktie swap in the men's dormitory at college one time. It was one of the most exciting and fun times we ever had. My roommate started out with nothing and ended up with six beauties!

The Bible talks about the greatest trade ever, in 2 Corinthians 5:21: "For he [God] hath made him [Jesus] to be sin for us, who knew no sin; that we might be made the righteousness of God in him." We could transpose the phrases just a bit, For God hath made Jesus, who knew no sin, to be sin for us; that we who knew no righteousness might be made the righteousness of God in Him.

How would you like to have Jesus, with His wide-open

arms and friendly eyes, walk up to you today and offer to trade all His righteousness for all your sins? Would you be interested? The truth is that this is exactly what He offers to do. It would appear at first that someone would end up with the small end of the deal. Not only is it like trading a Cadillac Seville for a ballpoint pen, there's no ballpoint pen! All we have to trade for His righteousness is a pile of filthy rags. Yet that is precisely what the salvation trade is all about. It's the greatest trade ever. How can it be? You again come up with the same conclusion. Either the One who offers to make this trade is very foolish, or else He really loves us a lot.

And yet we have a problem. One of the questions that is heavily debated today among church people and theologians is this: When Jesus gives us His gift of righteousness, does He really give it to us? Is it a trade? Or does He loan it to us? Does He really make *us* righteous, or does He simply declare us righteous? How do you fit this all together? Is it a trade, a gift, or a loan?

When Jesus gives us His righteousness, is it permanent or temporary? Theologians have often discussed the question, If God forgives our sins now, but we are lost someday in spite of it, what happens to the sins that were once forgiven? Will He someday raise all of them back out of the depths of the sea and bring them against us?

Is a trade always permanent? Not in human understanding! My boy traded his old MG for another boy's Honda 350. Neither boy was happy, and they traded back again. When you borrow something, you are expected to pay it back. But wait a minute—if Jesus' righteousness is loaned to us, what do we have to pay Him back with? So maybe it really is a gift. But is it permanent or not?

I hope I am at least managing to stir up your pure minds to the question at hand! How do you answer? I'd like to suggest an answer by going into a bit of word study on the question of righteousness. Daniel 9:7 says that righteousness belongs to God, but to us, confusion of face. When we look around in this world of sin for any kind of righteousness among people, we end up with nothing but confusion. The Bible principle is that man is bankrupt of righteousness. We have none. Romans 3:10, 11: "It is written, there is none righteous, no, not one: there is none that understandeth, there is none that seeketh after God." Isaiah 64:6 says that "all our righteousnesses," anything that we have ever thought of as righteousness, "are as filthy rags." So there is nothing more critical and more significant in all Bible teaching than that even though we might be able to produce something that the world calls morality, there is no such thing as righteousness as far as God is concerned. We may produce external goodness, but external goodness is not righteousness, and it doesn't count with God.

So the apostle Paul makes a sweeping statement that Jesus came to declare, not our righteousness, but the righteousness that is by faith in Jesus Christ. Romans 3:22. He repeats it several times. Verses 26, 27: "To declare . . . his righteousness: that he might be just, and the justifier of him which believeth in Jesus. Where is boasting then? It is excluded."

If there is no such thing as righteousness as far as we are concerned, but if the Lord knows the way of the righteous (Psalm 1:6) and there is to be a resurrection of the righteous (Luke 14:14) and the righteous are going to shine as the sun in their Father's kingdom (Matthew 13:43), then there must be some way that righteousness can be known by poor sinners who are bankrupt of it. But it must be known in such a way that there is no boasting and no credit and no merit for producing it, right? "Where is boasting . . . ? It is excluded."

The Bible gives us a grasp of the gospel and how this is possible. According to 1 Corinthians 1:30, Jesus "is made unto us wisdom, and righteousness, and sanctification, and redemption." We also have Paul's famous statement in Romans 1:16, 17 that the gospel of which he is not ashamed is the gospel, or the good news, of Jesus Christ, "for therein is the righteousness of God revealed from faith to faith." In the good news about Christ, the righteousness of God is revealed. So as you trace through this key word, righteousness, you discover that we have none, that God has it all, and that it has been revealed to this world through Jesus Christ.

The greatest single definition of righteousness is Jesus. Simply defining it as right doing is inadequate, even though some of us did that for a long time. We said, "Righteousness, what is that? That's right doing. All right then, the logical conclusion is that if righteousness is right doing, then all we have to do to become righteous is to do what's right." This led many of us into the trap of wasting time and effort trying to do what is right in order to be righteous.

Now, although it is true that in a sense righteousness can be defined in terms of right doing, this is not all there is to the definition. The Bible truth is that righteousness is never existent apart from Jesus. It comes with Jesus. When Paul says in 1 Corinthians 1:30 that Jesus "is made unto us wisdom, and righteousness, and sanctification, and redemption," he means that in Jesus all of these things exist and are found.

One day we were talking about this and someone said, "Oh, that's good news. Let's pray for wisdom."

No! Let's pray for Jesus.

"Well," they said, "He will give us wisdom."

No, He gives us Himself, and wisdom comes with Him. It isn't that He gives us wisdom as an entity in itself. Wisdom is never separated from Jesus—it comes with Him, in Him.

It is the same with righteousness. The righteousness of God is embodied in Christ. If we don't receive Christ for righteousness, we don't have any righteousness. It is never known apart from Him.

Sometimes the question is asked, Is righteousness infused? Well, in the first place, what is meant by that? While I was attending a meeting in Australia a man jumped up in the back of the room and said, "Do you believe that righteousness is infused?" He had a bit of fire in his eye and evidently had gotten the impression from the way I had been talking that I believed in "infused" righteousness.

I had to find out what he meant.

He said, "Do you believe that righteousness is an entity in itself, something that you can pour into the individual and he can have it from that point on?"

I asked, "Apart from Christ?"

"Yes."

I said, "No."

But apparently when you hear the term "infused" righteousness, the person is indicating a sort of entity in itself that can be known apart from Christ. I do not believe in infused righteousness, because righteousness is never independent of Jesus Christ.

Well, then if this is true, does Christ's righteousness ever become inherently my own? Back to our text again on the greatest trade ever, 2 Corinthians 5:21. Notice it a little more carefully this time. "For he [God] hath made him [Jesus] to be sin for us." What does that mean? When Jesus became sin for us, did this ever make Him a sinner? Did Jesus become sinful when He became sin for us? First Peter 2:22 says He "did no sin, neither was guile found in his mouth." Jesus Himself successfully challenged a hostile audience: "Which of you convicts me of sin?" John 8:46, RSV. So when Jesus became sin for us, He was not a sinner. He took the penalty of our sins, He took the condemnation, He somehow took the guilt; but He never took the responsibility for sin. That's why there is a scapegoat at the end of the sanctuary service. See Leviticus 16. The devil has always been the one responsible for sin. Jesus bore our sins in terms of condemnation and penalty and guilt, and we can say that our sins were put to His account. But that never made Him a sinner.

Now follow through to the last half of the text. Second Corinthians 5:21: "That we might be made the righteousness of God in him." When we are made the righteousness of God in Him, that doesn't make *us* righteous any more than the other made Him sinful. When Christ becomes our righteousness, that doesn't make us righteous any longer than we are in Christ and with Christ. The righteousness is not inherently our own; it is only and always in Jesus. Sinful man can find hope and righteousness only in God, and no human being is righteous any longer than he has faith in God and maintains a vital connection with Him.

Let's get back to the Cadillac Seville. Let's say that I now own a brand new Cadillac Seville and I'm single. (That's the only way I could own one!) I'm looking for someone to ride around in my Cadillac Seville with me. For life! Now, of course, this can get a little tricky, because there's always the danger that she will be more interested in my Cadillac Seville than in the one who owns it. I hope I don't get that kind of person, so I go on looking until I find someone who apparently is more interested in me than in the Cadillac Seville. Albeit, when she marries me, she gets a Cadillac Seville; and ideally when she says, "I do," she says it permanently and will not renege on the arrangement.

When I accept Jesus as my Saviour, my Lord, and my Friend, I have all of His righteousness, because His righteousness comes with Him. Now if my new bride should someday decide that she no longer wants me (and don't confuse this with the marriage laws in your state—I am describing my own laws this time!), she no longer has the Cadillac Seville.

Was the Cadillac a loan? Was it a gift? Was it a trade? The Bible calls righteousness a gift (Romans 5:17), but righteousness is a gift in the same way that Jesus is a gift. I must continue to receive Him as a gift on a daily basis. It is possible, because of the power of choice, for me someday to choose not to have Jesus and all of the gifts that He brings with Him. When I do that, I no longer have any righteousness. Does this make sense?

Therefore righteousness is never an entity in itself. Righteousness is not infused any more than Jesus is infused. The two are inseparable. I would like to go so far as to suggest that the two are inseparable, whether they are imputed or imparted. We make a lot of distinction these days on that, but righteousness and Jesus are inseparable on both fronts. You receive righteousness in the imputed sense only by receiving Jesus, and you receive righteousness in the imparted sense only by receiving Jesus. They operate the same way, by the same method, all the way through, and you have to have Jesus to get either one.

But, you know, it does seem as if someone really ends up on the small end of the horn, namely the One who offers all of His righteousness for all of my sins. He must really love us, for we cannot attribute foolishness to God. He really must love us to make this kind of offer, just as you'd really love me to trade your Cadillac for my ballpoint pen. But doesn't He end up being cheated? To answer, I'd like to resurrect an old story—the story of Old Joe.

Old Joe was a slave down at the other end of the Mississippi, and he was on the auction block. He had determined that he would never work again. The bidders began to bid, and Joe began to mutter under his breath at first, and then louder and louder, "I won't work. I won't work." He was heard, and one by one the bidders dropped off, except for one man, who traded good money for this slave who wouldn't work.

The new master took Joe to his carriage and drove out into the country to his plantation. Finally he went down the road past a little lake. Beside the lake was a beautiful cabin with curtains on the windows and flowers by the steps. Joe had never seen anything like it. He said, "This is where I'm going to live?"

"Yes."

"But I won't work."

Then the master said, "Joe, you don't have to work. I bought you to set you free."

The best part of the story is still to come. Joe fell at the feet of his new master and said, "Master, I'll serve you forever."

You see a group of sinners. They have been slaves to sin and pain and death. They say, "We won't work, we *can't.*" Have you ever tried it? Have you ever tried to produce the works of righteousness? It's impossible. You can't do it. But Jesus says, "*You* don't have to work. I've bought you with My own blood to set you free."

I understand He has some mansions by a lake that looks like a sea made out of glass. There are cobblestones and curtains and flowers like you've never seen, flowers that will never fade. He offers us all of this because He loves us. That's the way He is. In the end, when we understand this trade and it really gets through to our hearts, we will gladly serve Him forever.

God's Enemy, the Devil

When my brother and I were small, we got into the routine of praying the same prayer every night, "Dear Lord, help us not to have bad dreams, help us not to think about war, and help the devil not to jump in the window." We were sincere. However, as we grew older, I can still remember the night we repeated our prayer and suddenly burst out laughing! We felt terribly blasphemous at the time, but apparently age was catching up with us, and we recognized it as a rather naïve prayer.

There are people today who think it is naïve to believe in the devil. But I confess that I knew there was a devil by experience long before I knew there was a God by experience. If you don't realize sooner or later that there's someone else in control, then you are naïve indeed. Let's take a look at the Bible teaching on the subject.

Two classic chapters in the Old Testament come to mind, Ezekiel 28 and Isaiah 14. You might add to that from the New Tesatment, Revelation 12. There you find some heavy teaching on the matter of the devil. Let's begin with Ezekiel 28.

At first glance it may appear that the devil isn't even mentioned. But if you look again, under the symbol of the king of Tyre we find something about the devil. Notice verse 13: "Thou hast been in Eden the garden of God." Was the king of Tyre ever in Eden? "Every precious stone was thy covering." Verse 14: "Thou art the anointed cherub that covereth." Did the king of Tyre qualify for that? Obviously not. "Thou wast upon the holy mountain of God; thou hast walked up and down in the midst of the stones of fire." Verse 15: "Thou wast perfect." Does the king of Tyre qualify for that? "Thou wast perfect in thy ways from the day that thou wast created, till iniquity was found in thee." So we have here a passage that most Bible commentaries agree is clearly indicating the devil himself and his history.

Notice as you read on, verse 17: "Thine heart was lifted up because of thy beauty, thou hast corrupted thy wisdom by reason of thy brightness." The devil today doesn't always go into the gutter to bring up the scum and mire. He knows how to use beauty. He is familiar with wisdom and brightness. Don't picture him with flames shooting out of his nostrils, and a split tongue and a pitchfork tail. He knows how to use position. He came from the dizzy heights. So you can learn from this passage a bit of the history of Lucifer, son of the morning.

Obviously the devil lives and operates in a realm that we cannot see. I have always been intrigued since the mathematics professor drew it on the board, giving me evidence from the Bible that the angels and God and even the devil himself operate in another dimension than the one we are in. The most we know are three dimensions. The devil must be operating in at least the fourth dimension, and probably God in a much higher dimension than that.

If we had been created in only two dimensions, he could be right on top of us in the third dimension and we couldn't see him, because we would only be operating in two directions. But we are in three dimensions. So God and the angels and even the devil could be right next to us, and we wouldn't see them if, as the mathematics teacher suggested, they really are in another dimension.

Mathematicians have no problem trying to fathom that, even though we can't, because math goes easily into multi-dimensions and can usually be proved theoretically.

We are aware without even going into the math of it that the devil and his angels operate in a dimension we can't get to. We cannot see them, we can't get them out in the open. The Bible says the angels are spirits. See Ephesians 6. The good angels are good spirits, and the fallen angels are fallen spirits.

When you turn to Isaiah 14, the other Old Testament passage that deals with the devil, you find that he is actually named. He is mentioned in connection with Babylon, which, as you know, goes back to the Tower of Babel and is a classic example of mankind trying to save itself, trying to live on its own apart from God. This was the issue with Lucifer in the very beginning. Isaiah 14:12 and onward: "How art thou fallen from heaven, O Lucifer, son of the morning! how art thou cut down to the ground, which didst weaken the nations!"

Then God gives us, from heaven's viewpoint, what went on in the mind and thinking of this being. "Thou hast said in thine heart, I will ascend into heaven, I will exalt my throne above the stars of God: I will sit also upon the mount of the congregation, in the sides of the north: I will ascend above the heights of the clouds; I will be like the most High." Lucifer had I-trouble. In spite of his great wisdom he forgot that he was in an entirely different league than God was. He must have forgotten that he was a created being and that God was his Maker. Otherwise, how could he have thought he could be like the most High?

Did this attitude, which began with Lucifer, end with him? Can't we see the same kind of tendency in ourselves, to forget that we are creatures? It is only a very foolish creature that would think he could operate independent of his Maker.

But Lucifer continued to indulge his pride, and so you see developing a remarkable difference between Lucifer and the One who left the heavenly country to come to earth on an opposite mission. Sometime sit down and read Isaiah 14; then compare it with Philippians 2. Lucifer said, "I will be like God." Jesus said, "I will be like man." Lucifer said, "I will be exalted," but instead, he was brought down to hell to the sides of the pit. Jesus said, "I will be like man," and His Father said, "I will exalt Him."

Lucifer said, "I will bring fear. I will cause the nations to tremble because of my power." Jesus said, "I will bring love, and perfect love casts out fear." Lucifer said, "I will destroy the nations." Jesus, the Creator, said, " I will give them new hearts." Lucifer said, "I will take prisoners captive and will not open my prison house." Jesus said, "I will come and deliver the captives and set them free." Lucifer said, "I will deceive." Jesus said, "I am the way, the truth and the life." Lucifer said, "I will persecute and cause pain and sorrow." Jesus said, "I will bring deliverance." What a contrast! What a difference!

Well, let's take a look at how the devil has worked. We don't have to remind ourselves too much of that, as you are probably painfully aware. But, in one sense, it might appear that God has the advantage, because He's still in charge. But when we consider that in the great controversy God has never overstepped Himself but has conducted the whole controversy so fairly that someday even the devil is going to admit that He has been fair and just, then it looks as though the devil has the advantage. For the devil can lie and cheat, and apparently the one who can lie and cheat has the advantage. Have you ever, at some time in your life, thought you would have an advantage if you told a lie? But crooked lines always run into each other, and sooner or later the one who thinks he has the advantage of dishonesty meets himself coming back.

The devil has been miserable since the start of his rebellion. Separation from God always brings misery, always. That's why you have people running over each other in the great entertainment centers, trying to forget that they're miserable. In his misery, the devil determined to spread his misery to as many others as possible, and he is spreading misery everywhere today under the guise of fun, entertainment and so-called happiness.

But in the end, all this frantic fun ends in nothing but misery and heartache and emptiness and pain. When people come to realize that fact, the devil says, "Quick! Get busy!" He tries to keep people so busy that they will not have time to pause and think of God, their Maker and their Creator. So you find people in a constant whirl of activity, sometimes even religious activity, trying to keep busy enough to forget the fact that they are living apart from God.

Another method the devil has used is to try to get people to believe they don't need any restraints or commandments or laws or regulations. He tells them they can rely on their own wisdom. This was one of his arguments with the angels, back at the beginning of his rebellion, and he succeeded with one third of them.

He comes along with his freedom pitch and says to young people, "Do as you want. I'll give you freedom." You know how it went in the 60s, with rocks through university windows, buildings ransacked, and riots. It has happened in some form in every age. We've seen enough of it to know that in the end, instead of freedom there is slavery.

And how many people he has caused to take the downward path and then told them that God will never accept them, that they have gone too far. His two great arguments have always been, and always will be, first, that you can't overcome or obey; and second, that when you fail, you can't be forgiven. He charges God with his own attributes and tries to get people to think of God with the same distrust and fear they should feel when they think of the devil.

The devil uses condemnation and accusation and pressure as he tries to keep people under his control. You don't have to put people on the rack and stretch them apart, you don't have to burn them at the stake to create pressure that will cause them to cheat or steal or lie. You can even do it in a Christian setting. I remember a young people's meeting once when there was a Bible quiz, and the first ones who were able to answer the questions got to sit down. The last one standing was the loser. I still remember watching the face of the last little girl, as one by one all the others sat down and she was left standing alone. I said to myself, "This is of the devil." Sometimes we use force and pressure to accomplish what appears to be religious purposes. How subtle.

As you come to the age of the earth's history when it looks as if there isn't much time left, people find it easy to become preoccupied with the devil, and panic begins to rise. But I would like to remind you today that in the light of the mighty power of Jesus, there is no need for panic. The devil is nothing in His presence.

Now, I respect the devil. I hope you will interpret that word correctly. I respect him in the sense that I know he's bigger and more powerful than I am. I am not big enough to handle him; I am not cunning enough to outwit him. But I have learned that the devil, in spite of his rebellion, has a healthy respect for Jesus Christ. We have no reason to fear as long as we are in the presence of Jesus and under His protection.

Sometimes books are written, or some tapes will be circulated that talk about the power of the devil. People begin to panic. But I'd like to suggest that we have known for a long time that the devil is as a roaring lion and that he will continue to work with increased activity until the very end. Whether Jesus comes next year, or whether He comes

10,000 years from now, it should make no difference in our response of love to Him. If you are shaken up by whatever latest bit of panic is circulating, the least you can do is to take a long look at the cross. Let's become more interested in Jesus and what He has done for us than we are preoccupied with the devil.

There are Christians who talk and think altogether too much about the power of Satan. They think of their adversary, they pray about him, they talk about him, and he looms up greater and greater in their imagination. It is true that Satan is a powerful being, but thank God we have a mighty Saviour who cast out the devil from heaven. Satan is pleased when we magnify his power. Why not talk of Jesus, why not magnify His power?

Christ's followers are to look upon Satan as a conquered foe. Upon the cross Jesus gained the victory for them. The omnipotent power of the Holy Spirit is the defense of every contrite soul. Not one that in penitence and faith claims His protection will Christ permit to pass under the enemy's power. Isaiah 59:19: "When the enemy shall come in like a flood, the Spirit of the Lord shall lift up a standard against him."

The Christian, the one who has a vital relationship with Christ, has nothing to fear. But the one who chooses to live a life continually apart from the Lord Jesus, even though he may live that life in a religious community, has everything to fear. Let's transfer our fears onto the broad shoulders of Jesus Christ and come under His protection as He invites us to do.

Well, the devil also demonstrates something that is quite pronounced, even among human beings. At the very end, he comes down with great wrath, because he knows he has but a short time. See Revelation 12:12. When a person loses his composure and gets involved in wrath, he also loses his judgment. Have you ever noticed that?

I can remember a few fights I had a hundred years ago. My father always told me, "Any fool can fight. It takes a strong person, a real man, to stay out of a fight." I'm glad I didn't get into too many. But one or two still stand out in my memory. I lost my cool and I lost my judgment.

In the end, the devil loses his composure and his judgment and begins to do foolish things. He meets himself coming back. You can count on it.

Thank God, in spite of all the devil's efforts, his obituary notice is already printed in Scripture. This is good, but it is also sad. You can read about it in Ezekiel 28:18, 19: "I will bring thee to ashes upon the earth in the sight of all them that behold thee. All they that know thee among the people shall be astonished at thee: thou shalt be a terror, and never shalt thou be any more."

And read Isaiah 14:16, 17: "They that see thee shall narrowly look upon thee, and consider thee, saying, Is this the man that made the earth to tremble, that did shake kingdoms; that made the world as a wilderness, and destroyed the cities thereof; that opened not the house of his prisoners?" Is this the man?

Evidently the devil is going to come out of his dimension, and everyone will see him. Some will be on the inside of a city looking out; others will be on the outside of a city looking in. There, perhaps on a ledge somewhere, we will see him, with his huge frame, his forehead that recedes from his eyes, and the flesh that hangs loose from his face. We will see him struggling to his knees as from the force of his own awareness he admits that God has been fair and just in all His dealings. As people look at him through narrowed eyes they will say, Is this the man that made the nations tremble? Then, according to Scripture, fire will come down from God out of heaven and devour him. See Revelation 20.

For many years I have pondered this scene, trying to picture what it's going to be like. At first I thought the angels would sweep a note higher on their harps, and the trumpeters of heaven would blast their trumpets. I thought we'd all be singing and dancing and shouting and throwing our hats in the air.

Suddenly the picture changed. Because, if God is the kind of God I understand Him to be, I think the scene will be quite different. Lucifer was created by God. He was once one of His most shining creations. He was God's child.

In the early days, when a desperado was hanged, you could see a mother somewhere in the crowd, weeping her eyes out. When the devil is finally brought to ashes, I see the God of heaven, the Father of love, convulsed in sobs of anguish. God is the one who created Lucifer, and a son gone bad is a son still.

I see the angels stop their singing, as they begin to weep along with God. Perhaps we will weep too. Because, though it will be good news when he is gone, it is still bad news that he has to go.

God has no pleasure in the death of the wicked. What a challenge to be on the inside of that city and to join forever in the peace and happiness of fellowship with such a God of love.

We believe in the spiritual unity and mission of the church

A Lizard Can Grow a New Tail, but a Tail Can't Grow a New Lizard

A businessman asked his Christian friend, "Why can't a person be a Christian without joining a church?"

The Christian did not give an immediate answer. But a few days later the two men walked together past a church. "See that dark, dusty window?" asked the Christian.

"Yes, what about it?" said the businessman. "Nothing very inspiring about it that I can see."

"Let's see it from the inside," said the friend, as he led his companion through the open door into the church. Gone was the dark dullness of the outside view, for the afternoon sun was streaming through the window, gloriously lighting the stained-glass figure of Christ, the Good Shepherd. The man looked in silence at the brilliantly lighted face. Finally the Christian said, "Clearer, isn't it? There you have it. Christians join the church because one can see Jesus better from the inside."

Well, it's a nice story. It was used as an illustration in a Voice of Prophecy Bible course. But we might think of alternatives to that story, such as nighttime, when the church is lighted up, and it looks more glorious from the outside than from the inside! There has to be something better than a story to show the significance of the church. And there is—it is the authority of God's Word. However, I like the story nonetheless, and would like to think that Jesus is revealed better inside the church. Has that been your experience? Apparently it has been for some.

When we think of the church, we think of at least three aspects. First is the brick and mortar and stone—the physical building. People sometimes object to the amount of money spent on a costly sanctuary. They seem to forget about Solomon's temple and even the wilderness sanctuary. There was a lot of gold there! For what purpose are you spending the money and lavishing the wealth? Is it for God's glory, or your own? There can be a fine line between the two.

My brother preached a sermon at the dedication of the Mountain View, California, church that both he and I had a part in building. He chose for his text, "God . . . dwelleth not in temples made with hands." Acts 17:24. His point was that there is something more to a church than its physical struture. But sometimes we tend to dismiss the importance of the actual building. We can turn to John 2:16 and discover that Jesus drove the people out of the temple, out of the church of His day, and said, "Make not my Father's house an house of merchandise." So Jesus Himself had a tender regard for the church building which had been built for His Father's house.

Another aspect of the church is the organic church, the church organization. You might think of the Adventists and the Baptists and the Catholics and the Presbyterians. Or you might think of the local, organized church. But let's be sure that the Scripture talks about organic churches as well. Probably the best place to study this is the writings of Paul, who speaks again and again of the organized churches in various cities. He speaks of the groups of churches under the one heading called *church,* obviously referring to what we might call the *denomination* today. He refers to certain actions being taken at headquarters in Jerusalem. Revelation 1:12, 13, 20 reminds us of the seven churches, represented by the seven candlesticks.

The third aspect of the church is what many people are particularly interested in today—the mystical church, the universal church. It includes the faithful followers of God everywhere. For some who have become disenchanted with organized religion, the idea of the mystical church is very appealing.

Wherever I go, I meet people who tell me they believe in the church. But, they say, the church they believe in is the church universal. They tell me that Christ's church is composed of all the various denominations; they claim that the record of membership is kept in heaven and that no one really knows who are members of Christ's church except Christ Himself. When you ask them if they are members of a particular church, they say No, but they are members of the church universal.

Let's read John 10:16. Jesus is speaking. He's talking about Himself as the Good Shepherd, and He says, "Other sheep I have, which are not of this fold: them also I must bring, and they shall hear my voice; and there shall be one fold, and one shepherd."

What does this text say to you? Think it through carefully. If there are other sheep not of the fold that Jesus was speaking of, He wanted to bring them into it so that there would be one fold and one Shepherd. This indicates more than simply a mystical body. Otherwise, how could these sheep be His yet "not of this fold"?

Is there a mystical body of Christ? Yes. Does God have purposes for that mystical body? Evidently yes. But there is also a place for the organized church. Matthew 18 suggests it in verse 15 and onward: If your brother trespasses against you, go to him and tell him his fault. If he won't hear you, then take with you one or two more. And if he neglects to hear them, tell it unto the church. But if he neglect to hear the church, let him be unto thee as an heathen man and a publican. You are familiar with these instructions on how to deal with an erring brother. If God were speaking only of the mystical church, whose members are registered and known only in heaven, how would you know where to go and with whom to discuss the problem? It would be impossible. So the very reading of this passage suggests the truth that God has an organized church that people know enough about so they can take their problems to it.

Paul referred to the organized church when he instructed Timothy about officers in the church and how to choose church leaders.

There is another reason, based upon logic and common sense, which helps us understand why God would want to have an organized church. Have you ever, all by yourself, sent out a missionary? Have you ever owned and operated a school or a hospital? The cooperative effort of a group of people can do what a single person cannot do. So God is able to work through the church organization to spread the gospel far more widely than if each Christian worked alone. Of course, the danger on the other extreme would be to worship the institutions we have built and to allow institutionalism to thwart God's real purpose. There is a balance somewhere in between, and we must find it.

Looking at the early church we see an organized group of believers who went everywhere and turned the world upside-down. There was some strategy, yes, some planning and unified effort. At the same time, their power came from the Holy Spirit. God's work can't be done by strategy alone; neither does the Holy Spirit work simply on His own. We understand that there is a high degree of organization even among the angels and celestial beings in the heavenly country.

So when you are tempted to be upset with the church and want to throw it on the scrap heap, think twice. Be sure you first study what the Bible says on the subject of all three churches—physical, organic, and mystical.

Many misunderstand the purpose of the organized church. Some think that all that's needed is to attend week by week and do nothing more than that. (Or, even worse, to attend the physical church only once or twice a year, perhaps on Christmas and Easter.)

Another tragic misunderstanding leads a large number to think that membership in the organic church assures them of salvation. There are even some who think that as long as their names are on the church books, everything is under control. If for some reason their names are removed from the church books, they do everything they can to be reinstated, thinking that their eternal destiny is based on that. But membership in the organized church is only significant when membership in God's mystical church goes along with it. The two must go together.

For the person who is only a member of the organized church, the purpose of church attendance is generally to *get*. But for the one who is a member of the mystical church as well, the purpose of church attendance can be to *give*. Have you ever heard anyone say, "I'm not going to church anymore, because I don't get anything out of it"? He is advertising his own problem, isn't he? He is admitting that his primary purpose for church attendance is to get.

What was Jesus' primary purpose for going to church? What did He get? He got led out to the edge of town to be thrown off a cliff, that's what He got! If anyone deserved to stay home and read His Bible, it was Jesus. But He was always in church. If you want to see the significance Jesus places on the church, even the very inept church of His day, watch Him as He closes His carpenter's shop for the Sabbath and goes to the synagogue. Jesus went to give. Sometimes He was allowed more opportunity to give than others—and sometimes you are allowed more opportunities to give than others. But if you are looking for a chance to give, you will be able to find it. You may not always know when you are giving. Someday you may find out that when you least suspected it, someone else was discouraged, ready to give up, and saw you there and heard your amen and kept coming. It is possible to give by just a handshake or a smile.

In 1 Corinthians 12 Paul compares the church to the human body and talks about the different members. Maybe you are the hand or the eye or even the adrenaline! No matter which part of the body you are, it is true that when the tooth begins to suffer, every part of the body sympathizes with it. The foot runs along as fast as it can to bring the tooth to someplace where it may find relief. The hand reaches out to see if there is something that can be put onto the tooth to stop its aching. The eye looks around, searching for some remedy that can be applied. Every part of the body is in motion, trying to bring help to the suffering member.

When a person has a toothache, the hand doesn't say, "Well, I'm not going to bother with that tooth. It made a mistake eating too many sweets; let it tend to itself." The foot doesn't say, "I'm going to sleep. I am not going to worry about the tooth that is aching." No, all of the body becomes involved when any one of its members is in pain.

Once again, in the analogy of the body the organic church is strongly suggested, for if some member of the body of Christ whose name was known only in heaven were suffering, how would anyone else know about it? But when one member of the organized body is suffering, all the other members should, in every way possible, do their best to relieve that suffering. No one should be allowed to suffer alone. The fact that his suffering may be the result of his own sins is not sufficient reason to leave him to fight the battle alone. A little scratch on the hand, if given prompt attention, is soon healed. But a little scratch on the hand, if neglected by the rest of the members of the human body, may finally result in serious trouble. So in the Christian church. If all the members of the church would take an interest in even the small matters that affect its members, much sorrow could be avoided.

The analogy of the body tells us something else—a body is not a body unless it hangs together! Once in a while someone says, "I don't know why I have to go to church. I don't know why I can't just be a Christian in my own home. I get much more blessing. . . . I GET much more blessing out of walking in the woods or sitting by my fireplace reading."

On the basis of case histories, and on the basis of God's Word, I usually tell them, "Then you're going to die." It's a plain, cruel, painful fact. If you cut off your hand and leave it home by the fire or send it off for a walk in the woods, the hand is going to die. I have heard that if you cut off a lizard's tail, it will keep wiggling for a little bit—but not for very long. And although a lizard can grow a new tail, a tail can never grow a new lizard!

Well, you may say, why can't I be part of the body of Christ without going to church? You have to have unity of the body in practice before you have unity of the body in spirit. Even though we are not in church all through the week, when it is our custom and practice to be together as a corporate body on a regular basis and go through the pains and joys of life together, then we can operate in unity of spirit through the week as well. But if we never know what it's like to be together, to assemble to worship and share together, then it's very unlikely we will ever find unity of spirit and be a body in spirit, either.

Another thing you can learn from the body is that the body is organized. If it were not, there would be nothing but pandemonium. Can you imagine a disorganized human body? Picture what happens when the brain tells the hand to open the door and the hand doesn't obey. The face gets smashed! You would have all sorts of problems, wouldn't you? We can be thankful that the human body is organized, and this is analagous to the church.

Something else that a body does is to eat. What is it about the body that eats? Is it just the mouth? No, if you cut out a mouth and tell it to eat, it's not going to eat. All the body is involved together in the eating process. What do we do when we gather together as the body of Christ? We eat. John 6 talks about it. Jesus compared it to eating His flesh and drinking His blood. When we go to church, we eat of the Bread of Life. And our body breathes. Lamentations 3 talks about prayer and likens it to breathing. We, in a corporate body, in church every Sabbath, are involved in breathing. There's no life without breathing. There's no life without eating. A body also exercises. First Timothy 4:7, 8 refers to this. We know that Christian outreach and service to others is what the exercise of the soul is all about. So when we gather together as the body of Christ, we eat, we breathe, and we exercise. All three are necessary to life.

In Ephesians 4:11-13, after speaking in the first part of the chapter about one Lord, one faith, one baptism, Paul goes on to say that God gave to the church apostles, prophets, evangelists, pastors, and teachers, for a purpose—"For the perfecting of the saints, for the work of the ministry, for the edifying of the body of Christ: till we all come in the unity of the faith, and of the knowledge of the Son of God, unto a perfect man, unto the measure of the stature of the fulness of Christ."

God has a purpose for the body, His own analogy of the church. Christ loved the church (see Ephesians 5:25) and gave Himself for it. I believe that you will find the church significant even though you may also find hypocrites there. What a tragedy if we were to leave the body of Christ and miss the blessings of the body, simply because there were some hypocrites among its members.

They were giving away 40 free Cadillacs in San Francisco as an advertising gimmick. They were to be given to the first 40 people in line on Monday morning. I slept on the sidewalk the night before, and when the doors were about to open on Monday morning, I was among the first ten in line. My Cadillac Seville was assured.

Just then I looked behind me and saw among the others waiting for Cadillacs some real hypocrites. I said, "If they're going to give Cadillacs to *those* kinds of people, you can forget mine." I turned and walked away!

Do you get the message of this parable? Hasn't God's church often had people who, according to our understanding, maybe shouldn't have been members? Even in Jesus' own church there was Judas, and later Ananias and Sapphira. Let's never get bogged down with the problem of hypocrites in the church.

On the other hand, perhaps all of us could witness to something really significant we have gotten from the church, if we have been looking for it. I'll never forget spending a summer in San Francisco attending the state college to pick up a few credits. On my first Friday night back on the Christian college campus, sitting in a group of members of the body of Christ, I felt an overwhelming sense of relief and peace come over me. These were people with more or less devotion, but they were searching and seeking, interested in the things of God. It was a beautiful oasis.

How often we bypass the blessing and give such feeble excuses for doing so! Think of all the excuses some give for not going to church. Someone handed me a list one time under the caption of "Reasons I Do Not Go to the Movies." Listen to them. "I don't go to the movies because I don't like crowds. I don't go to the movies because I can't sit still very long. I don't go to the movies because they always ask for money. I don't go to the movies because no one speaks to me there. I don't go to the movies because I never seem to get a good seat. I don't go to the movies because there are a lot of hypocrites and sinners there. I don't go to the movies because the manager never comes to call on me. I don't go to movies because when I have time away from work, I need to sleep."

Perhaps we should change the analogy. Why don't you go to the ballgame? People go to ballgames in spite of the crowds. People go to ball games and sit for half a day. They sit in front of their TVs for hours at a time. The reason is that they are interested in what is happening there. They go in spite of the difficulties involved. Some of our reasoning doesn't make sense.

My final argument for going to church is that Jesus did. Luke 4:16: "He came to Nazareth, where he had been brought up: and, as his custom was, he went into the synagogue on the Sabbath day, and stood up for to read." Is that a good reason for going to church, because it was His custom? I think so.

Custom isn't all bad. It's a custom to eat. Is that bad? It's customary for husbands and wives to tell each other that they love each other. Is that bad? It's the custom of some people to go jogging every morning. Is that bad? It's a custom for the sun to shine. Is that bad? I'm glad some things are customary, aren't you?

Jesus went to the synagogue, as was His custom. Luke 4:17, 18: They "delivered unto him the book of the prophet Esaias. And when he had opened the book, he found the place where it was written, The Spirit of the Lord is upon me, because [1] he hath anointed me to preach the gospel to the poor; [2] he hath sent me to heal the broken-hearted, [3] to preach deliverance to the captives, [4] and recovering of sight to the blind, [5] to set at liberty them that are bruised."

What was Jesus doing here? He was back home where He had been brought up. Some people are in church today because that's how they were brought up. He began to read to the people. You can read it in your Bible. *To preach the gospel to the poor.* Why? Because too many rich people won't listen. The rich and increased with goods who have need of nothing don't want the gospel. *To heal the broken-hearted.* Why? Because it is the people who realize they are broken-hearted and need to be healed who will listen and understand and accept. *To preach deliverance to the captives.* Why? Because only those who realize they are imprisoned in a world of sin are open for the Son who can set them free. Those who think they are already free don't need that kind of message. And *recovering of sight to the blind.* Why? Because the lukewarm person who doesn't have eyesalve and can't see doesn't feel a need for the righteousness of Christ.

To set at liberty them that are bruised. Have you been bruised and beaten by the devil? Are you discouraged because of your sins? Have you been hostile to religion because you have felt guilty? Have you felt uncomfortable, sure that Jesus wouldn't accept you? Listen, friend. In John 6:37 Jesus said, "Him that cometh to me, I will in no wise cast out." What good news! He accepts you just as you are.

To preach the acceptable year of the Lord. I don't know what all that means, but I know that it means at least this much: The Lord is willing and able to accept you, this year, today. He loves to accept people just as they are.

Jesus went to church and preached those things. Do you know where He knew that would lead Him? Right down the rocky, rugged path to the cross. It almost happened that day. The crowd took Him to the brink of a precipice outside the church. But all through His life, Jesus continued to give and to serve and to reach out. And He went to church because He knew there were people there who needed what He had to give.

I invite you, my friend, to go to church for these good solid Bible reasons—and receive what Jesus wants to give you today.